Accident and Deception
The Huey Long Shooting

By
Donald A. Pavy, M.D.

To Jo + Bill cousins + great people

Don Pavy

Cajun Publishing
2408 Darnall Road
New Iberia, LA 70560

Cover art: "What Really Happened"
By Anne Logan

Dedicated to my dear brother, the late Judge Henry Garland Pavy, who encouraged and aided in this endeavor and to my devoted wife, Yvonne Foret Pavy.

Editors: Don and Suzi Thornton

Acknowledgments:
I wish to express special thanks to Dr. Tom Ed Weiss, Dr. Carl A. Weiss, Jr. and Ida Pavy Boudreaux. This book would not have been possible without the letters, videos, newspaper clippings, photographs and personal communications so generously afforded me. They all were blessed to have loved Dr. Carl A. Weiss, Sr. and his wife, Yvonne. I hope this book does justice to their memories.

I acknowledge and thank many who aided with the writing of this book. I especially appreciate the support and help from Alfred Smith Landry, Michael Wynne, Earline Garber, and Claire Mire.

Foreword

"All the world's a stage and we are all but players in it."
                                                    Shakespeare

On September 8, 1935, something happened in the
Louisiana State Capitol building that tragically affected two
families, changed the course of 20th century Louisiana history, and has led to endless debate and study for many individuals for nearly three quarters of a century. Two men were
shot there, one dying at the scene and the other man possibly
mortally wounded. This event took place in front of, or near
the vicinity of, many members of the media, and the highest
ranking members of government, including law enforcement
and judiciary. Aside from all of these varied witnesses, one
of the victims lived for almost two days after the shooting
and was able to give sporadic, but useful, often "deathbed"-
quality testimony of the shooting. Some physical evidence
was at the scene of the shooting such as spent bullets, as well
as the numerous guns that fired the bullets, and the physical
damage done at the shooting scene. Additional critical evidence could have been revealed through autopsies of the victims as well as detailed treatment records of the surviving
victim.
   Both individuals were well known locally, one was
nationally (if not internationally) known and considered by
many as the third most photographed individual of the world
in that decade. The other individual, although young and not
so nearly well known, was a professional with a well-estab-
lished reputation and record of conduct in the community.
Although the shooting site building was a new structure, it
was probably one of the most publicly accessible sites to every citizen of the state for them to view the site of the shooting. The individuals in charge of determining treatment conditions for the surviving shooting victim had unlimited access and availability to the finest equipment and medical staff

that was available in 1935. The individuals in charge of investigating for the Louisiana government were the highest ranking and most knowledgeable law enforcement and judiciary figures in state and local government at that time. Additionally, as one of the victims was a high-ranking and prominent member of the federal government and a likely candidate for the office of President of the United States, the resources of the Federal Government were not only available upon request for investigative purposes, but were legally mandated (according to one opinion) for this investigation into the resolution of facts.

In the 64 years since the shooting, numerous individuals from all walks of life unconnected to the incident have conducted their own various investigations into the shooting using their own expertise and availability of evidence and testimony, and have generally added to the body of knowledge on this incident, an incident that actually lasted less than 30 seconds. So why, with all of the individuals and resources that were available, did this incident become the most biased, convoluted, and questionable investigation in American history? Why is this event still the most hotly debated event in Louisiana history, even more than when it originally occurred on September 8, 1935?

Doctor Donald A. Pavy, for the first time since the event occurred, looks at the shooting through the eyes of a medical doctor, a professional "detective" of sorts, and tries to diagnose what really happened on that fateful night in Louisiana history. Using the coolness of the passage of time, Doctor Pavy has reviewed, unemotionally and systematically, all known facts and purported facts, the motives of all the participants, and the physical and testimonial evidence. He puts it together as best as anyone will ever be able to as to who, what, when, where, why, and how. Although 64 years have passed since the original event, Doctor Pavy has miraculously discovered much new, relevant, and fascinating information and evidence into this historic shooting, an accomplishment by itself, worthy of reading and study by all. This book will be the last of its kind as no potential future author can eclipse what has been accomplished here.

Who killed Huey Long? And why? Doctor Pavy sorts out the various actors, stage settings, and script changes in this multi-act play. He reminds the public to open their minds and not just accept as fact what is performed in front of them on the stage of life. Doctor Pavy's book will change our history books and our minds on the single most momentous event in Louisiana history. He reminds us that just because history is written by the victors, the truth can still be determined by the readers.

Michael D. Wynne

Introduction
Accident and Deception
The Huey Long Shooting

"Truth crushed to earth shall rise again"
The Battlefield - Wm. Cullen Bryant

Accident and Deception is intended to be the definitive book on the shooting and death of Huey Pierce Long. It is being written after painstaking research and thorough analysis of all evidence available, including not only newly discovered information but also evidence which has gathered dust over the past 64 years.

On September 8, 1935, in a corridor leading from the Governor's office in the Louisiana State Capitol in Baton Rouge, Louisiana, a shooting occurred which resulted in the immediate death of Dr. Carl A. Weiss, a Baton Rouge physician, whose body was riddled with bullets. Huey P. Long, a U.S. Senator from Louisiana and former Governor of that state, died later as a result of complications from the bullet wound received in the shooting.

Accident and Deception was written to examine information and statements of witnesses and others concerned with the shootings of Senator Huey Long and Dr. Carl Weiss on September 8, 1935. This was the most important historical event in twentieth century Louisiana.

One important characteristic of physicians is an unquenchable curiosity. Each case presents a mystery. Medical knowledge and gathering of facts and information are used to solve diagnostic and therapeutic problems. A similar curiosity has been the driving force that has had me research and study the medical and non-medical aspects of the death of Huey Long.

As a general practitioner for nearly half a century, I have seen exciting progress in the medical arts and have learned much about medicine and human nature. In seeking the best information in the Huey Long shooting, I have sought advice from coroners, radiologists, surgeons, cardiologists, ballistic experts, and forensic pathologists. All this professional advice from experts in their fields, combined with my training, allows me to draw certain conclusions about this case never previously made with so much evidence.

In recent years more information has come forward to completely change the accepted belief that Huey Long was assassinated. I use this later information along with what has been known and accepted. Of great interest are the conflicting medical statements. At one time I thought it was possible that Dr. Weiss could have shot Huey. Now, with overwhelming information from different sources, I feel the mystery is finally solved. It can be said that any specific presentation, information or statement may be accused of being in error or is hearsay. However, the overwhelming amount of evidence tilts strongly against assassination.

There are many books and articles written about Huey Long. The following are some of interest in relation to his shooting and death.

The Huey Long Murder Case by Herman Deutch concludes that Weiss most likely shot Huey Long. Mr. Deutch was a close observer of Huey Long; he was present for his first speeches and was often in the presence of Huey, even visiting him in his home. Deutch's work, a pioneer effort, was too close to the event and persons involved to truly open up the case.

The Day Huey Long Was Shot, by David H. Zinman, leaves doubt as to whether Dr. Weiss actually shot Huey Long. Zinman devoted much of his effort showing, for the first time, the Weiss side of the incident. This was first published in 1963 and reprinted in 1993.

A Requiem for A Kingfish by Ed Reed was written at a later time with new "finds" in the case, that is, the remarkable story of a witness who was a parolee and thus not a political tie-in. His family passes down a story that contradicts the "official version." Reed concludes that Long was accidentally shot by his own bodyguards. Reed's work, masterfully done, produced the first great analysis of the shooting.

Thomas Angers, in the monthly *Acadiana Profile* explains information obtained by Colonel Francis Grevemburg, former Superintendent of State Police. Grevemberg states in an affidavit that bodyguards told him that Senator Long was accidentally shot by his own bodyguards.

Other books are mostly biographies. One is *The Kingfish and His Realm* by William Ivy Hair. Hair believes Senator Long was shot twice, once by Dr. Weiss and once by a bodyguard. Hair critiques the extensive biography *Huey Long* by T. Harry Williams, who was his former history teacher at LSU. In his biographical essay about Williams Hair writes: "Williams concedes that the Kingfish loves power and eventually became obsessed with it. Yet offering excuses for most of his actions, he credits Long with sincerity of purpose. In the opinion of this writer, Williams was overly sympathetic to Huey Long."

Lloyd Ratcliff, whose pen name is "Duel Stone," wrote a historical novel, *Conspiracy Unveiled*, the most recent book of relevance on the subject of the death of Huey Long. It contains no court or hospital records nor any affidavits and is based solely on anecdotal evidence. The author's claim is that his aunt learned of a conspiracy planned in a Baton Rouge grocery-pool hall involving a bodyguard, a doctor, and agents of business and government. In this unlikely scenario a drawing of lots was held and, by prior agreement, it fell to the person drawing the blank paper to assassinate Huey Long. Supposedly the doctor drew the blank paper and was to carry out the assassination. Simple as that. According to the story the aunt was later committed for life to a mental hospital in Washington, D.C. and never allowed to have visitors.

Encyclopedias, history books, and standard reference materials all state that Senator Huey Long was assassinated. If there is a place for justice in this world, history may have to be revised to record the truth about the death of Huey Long. That is why *Accident and Deception* was written, and this is my story.

Chapter I

Family Remembrances

Dr. Carl Austin Weiss was married to my first cousin, Yvonne Pavy. She was the daughter of Judge Benjamin Henry Pavy, a strong anti-Long leader in St. Landry Parish. Dr. Weiss has long been considered Huey Long's assassin. Think for a moment, if, indeed, he was not the assassin and Huey was shot accidentally, then an unbelievable deception has occurred for years. The consequences of Dr. Weiss being called an assassin have had great significance to both the Weiss and Pavy families, and still far greater for his widow, Yvonne, and son, Carl.

Yvonne Pavy Weiss left Louisiana after her husband's death and never wanted her son to know about the circumstances surrounding it. To this end, she lived in France for a time until World War II, then later reared Carl, Jr., in New York. A shock came to the young boy at the age of 10 when he saw the grotesque scene of the shooting of his father depicted on the cover of <u>Life</u> magazine.

Yvonne was a teacher of French with an advanced degree in foreign languages and wanted Carl to be educated in French. Throughout grammar and high school, Carl went to a school where all lessons were taught in French. He became an orthopedic surgeon studying in Boston, New York, and London. He is now semi-retired. Like his father, he has a fine intellect and is fluent in several languages.

The earliest recollection I have of any event in my entire life was when I was four years old. It was the day after Huey Long was shot. I was leaving my grandmother's home when I heard the adults in the car talking about the shooting. Our family was involved, I learned, but I didn't exactly understand in what way or know the details. Some time later, possibly within a week or two, I went with my father to visit my cousins. My father, Albert Pavy, was a country doctor.

He very often took me on calls in the country with him. We went to the home of my father's brother, Judge Henry Pavy, in Opelousas, but he was not at home. Marie and Evelyn, my cousins, both spinsters and much older than I, were there. A discussion of the horrors of all that had happened ensued. I remember in particular the two of them discussing the emptying of guns into the lifeless corpse of Dr. Weiss. My cousins felt that this was brutal. The news was, of course, quite frightening to a four-year-old. It left me filled with horror and I was terrified of this for a long time.

My father was never involved in politics; rather, his energies were depleted by a large medical practice, eight children, and a small farm and dairy. The latter was needed to help support his family. During the 1920's and 1930's few people had money to pay physicians. My father's car was always known as the "Stinker" by the children because he carried dairy products to and from the farm and they sometimes spilled. He had graduated from the University of Pennsylvania Medical School and studied tropical medicine at Johns Hopkins Medical School. He was a devoutly religious person, often saying his rosary on house calls.

My father had three brothers involved in politics in St. Landry Parish. They were Dr. Octave Pavy, Judge Benjamin Henry Pavy, and Paul Pavy. Paul was the principal of Opelousas High School, but was ousted by opposing political forces. My cousin, Marie Pavy, daughter of Henry, at the same time lost her position as a teacher in Opelousas. She was later reinstated and taught me.

Dr. Octave Pavy (Uncle Bill), who was older than my father, practiced in the horse and buggy days of medicine. What a character he was! My younger brother was named after him. Uncle Bill ran for Lieutenant Governor on Oramel H. Simpson's ticket which opposed Huey Long in 1927 when Huey was elected the governor. Uncle Bill later was in the State Legislature. He was very articulate and had a beautiful command of both the French and English languages, and had a warm way with people. He was the official spokesman for the family after the shootings. He lived in Leonville, a short distance from Opelousas, and for almost the entire first half of the twentieth century was the only source of medical care in that large area of St. Landry Parish which includes Melville, Port Barre to Arnaudville, and to Opelousas. As a child I loved to listen to my uncle and father discuss medical cases. In particular, I remember their elation in the late 1930's because of the advent of sulfa drugs. They were amazed that they could now cure pneumonia, gonorrhea, and other infections. They treated typhoid, yellow fever, malaria, polio and many other diseases that present day doctors have never seen. I recall his discussion about delivering babies by lamplight with chloroform out in rural areas. Uncle Bill related how he handled most difficult obstetrics such as an internal rotation of the infant to facilitate delivery. He had the husband or a family member administer anesthesia by pouring chloroform on a folded handkerchief. Today, Caesarean sections are always used for cases such as this. During the 1927 flood, my father and Uncle Bill worked tirelessly to care for refugees brought to elevated areas in Opelousas, La.

Dr. Octave Pavy knew Huey Long very well and once debated him in the 1928 race when Oramel Simpson was unable to appear. Forceful and never restrained by humility, he claimed to have won the debate and was told so by a priest in attendance. Uncle Bill stated on several occasions that he thought that Huey never believed there were people who possessed virtues, or even any degree of virtue. Acting on this, he controlled people much like the stock market, by fear and greed. Uncle Bill always recognized Huey's great intellect, but held him in contempt for his ethics. I always thought it strange that Uncle Bill used many profane words, considering his great vocabulary made it unnecessary. My parents would never use these words in our presence and pounced on us if we did so. My father, however, did use profanity, but only in French.

Uncle Bill was quite obese, but practiced medicine until a few months before his death in his eighties. He loved good food and often treated us to dinner in Lafayette and New Orleans. Uncle Bill was most kind to my mother, who was widowed young and had modest means with which to deal with her eight children, then ranging in age from twenty-two to five years. Most of us borrowed money for education from Uncle Bill. One thing I thought amusing was when he'd encounter the patient who did not or could not understand or was doubtful of the diagnosis or treatment, he would place his index finger on the person's forehead after saying that he was so glad the patient asked that question because he recognized the patient was very intelligent and could understand the medical complexities of the case. He then went on to explain the problem. Then he asked the patient if he understood or agreed. They would rarely disagree for fear of being thought stupid.

Uncle Bill was named after his uncle, another Dr. Octave Pavy, who was also a very interesting character. He and my grandfather were born in New Orleans and were educated in France before and during the Civil War. The first Dr. Octave Pavy was a captain in the Franco-Prussian War. He had an almost insane, burning desire to discover the North Pole. However, tragedy was his lot. Forty thousand dollars of his inheritance from his father was invested in an expedition to the North Pole. The night before sailing, his boat burned in the San Francisco Bay. Also, that night, his only financial backer was murdered by his valet. Whether these incidences were connected was never known. Penniless, but undeterred, Dr. Pavy became a civilian contract physician on an ill-fated army expedition to the Arctic. This in itself is another story. Lost, frozen, and starving, only six survived. Dr. Pavy died only a few weeks before the group was rescued and he was cannibalized.

Much has been written about my other uncle, Judge Benjamin Henry Pavy, Uncle Henry. Uncle Henry and my father were extremely close. My father was not only his brother but also the doctor for Uncle Henry's family. He treated some of the family through critical illnesses, staying with them night and day. They always had great respect and love for my father. Uncle Henry strongly opposed Huey Long in St. Landry Parish, where Huey lacked political strength. Huey's political fortune was stalemated there and this pushed him to pass a law to redraw the districts. Huey then appointed the judge and district attorney. Therefore Uncle Henry, who had held the office by election for twenty-five years, no longer had an office. Lee Garland, the district attorney who served for forty years, was my maternal great uncle. He was also gerrymandered out of office. Uncle Henry, I recall, was a large jovial man who would wet a nickel (big money in those days) and stick this to his forehead. Kids would sit on his lap and hug and kiss him for the coin.

One often told family story, which happened when I was very young, concerned my four older brothers. They were playing in the woods near some hunters. One brother, Henry Garland, or "Guffy," fell down and cried that he was shot. Some of the children, believing this, ran to town and related that Guffy had been shot. News spread fast, but no one had told my mother. Uncle Henry dismissed the court and rushed to our home with an entourage. About this time it was learned that Guffy was not shot. My mother was bathing and locked in the bathroom. This crowd knocked on the door, reassuring her Guffy was indeed not shot. This was shocking to my mother and she became weak. The door was forced open and my grandmother, who was a very tiny lady and probably equally upset, mistook machine oil for Spirits of Ammonia and gave this to my mother. Guffy later became a judge, reclaiming the same seat Long had taken away from Uncle Henry.

The Pavys were not, in Huey's early political years, anti-Long. They were, I suppose, populists. My grandfather, Alfred Pavy was once a wealthy cotton broker from New

Orleans and had been educated abroad. He married my grandmother, Laperle Guidry, who was from the Grand Coteau area.
The depression in the latter part of the Nineteenth Century
destroyed his business and left him penniless. He worked as
a laborer for the Jesuits at Grand Coteau to support his ten
children. Two sons became doctors. One of these sons, my
father, worked as a teacher to help pay for his education. Two
sons became lawyers, one became an engineer and one became a school principal. My grandfather accepted his im-
poverished state with dignity. Years later he became Clerk of
Court in Opelousas

My tiny maternal grandmother, of "machine oil" fame,
was a Garland by birth. Her brother, Lee Garland, had been
District Attorney in St. Landry Parish for over forty years.
The Garlands were from Virginia and were rather wealthy,
aristocratic, and well educated for their time. Lee Garland
and his brother, Henry "Yi" Garland Jr., were both graduates
of Manhattan College Law School. "Yi" was a prominent
lawyer in New Orleans and wrote a law book on practices
and procedures, which was used as a text in the early 1900's.
Lee opposed Huey from the very beginning. Uncle Lee probably rejected Huey more than most of Huey's opponents.
Once Huey visited Uncle Lee in his office in St. Landry Parish. Lee asked Huey who were the people accompanying
him. Long replied that they were his bodyguards. Lee requested they leave the room, which they did. Huey then proposed that Lee become his leader and ally in St. Landry Parish. The governor assured Uncle Lee that his two sons could
be given positions in state government with promised ad-
vancement. The older District Attorney became infuriated
and related to Huey that his wife had died when his seven
children were young and that he had tried hard to raise and
educate them properly. Becoming even more irate, he assured Huey he wanted no part of his proposal and said before
he would have his sons be influenced by Huey he would rather
shoot them himself. Lee then told Huey to get out of his of-

18

fice. This is an example of the political polarization and animosity of those days.

Kitty Halphen Prather relates the story that Huey called her grandfather, Lee Garland, to offer him the position of Assistant District Attorney just before Lee was put out of office by Huey's gerrymandering. Lee's phone reply was, "Go to hell, Huey!" and he promptly hung up. It was thought that Huey was reluctant to gerrymander Uncle Lee and Uncle Henry. The local "Long" people forced Huey's hand. The governor even tried not to alienate Uncle Lee, a rare move by Huey who cared little to placate opponents. I believe Huey felt Lee and Yi could cause him legal problems. Huey had probably studied the Garland law text.

Huey and Uncle Henry once had a fiery meeting in the judicial chambers in Opelousas. Uncle Henry was the recipient of Huey's choicest vulgarities. Nothing is known of the details of this meeting.

One tragic episode involved Gilbert Dupre, my mother's paternal uncle. Once a judge, he served in the legislature and was an early opponent of Huey. He later came on hard times and capitulated to Huey. He was old and deaf, and was teased about his change of political persuasion. He became enraged with Charlie Dejean one day, pulled a pistol and shot him to death near the courthouse in Opelousas. Austin Fontenot, a Long leader in the parish, successfully defended Dupre and he was acquitted. Huey later appointed Austin Fontenot District Attorney to replace Lee Garland.

To further illustrate how politics cut across family lines in those days, my father's sister, Blanche, was married to Dudley Guilbeau. The Guilbeau family was very strongly pro-Long.

Uncle Henry Pavy and Uncle Lee Garland were gerrymandered out of office by the Long forces in 1935. After that, the political influence of my family quickly declined. At present (1999) there is only one distant relative in government, City Judge Kenneth Boagni, Jr.

There is a humorous story told about those times. Veazie Pavy, son of Henry, and a few other anti-Longs once went to Palmetto, Louisiana, in St. Landry Parish, for a political rally. They began to speak from a parked wagon on the street. Soon after they began the crowd dispersed, except for one lone soul. They asked this person why he stayed when the others parted. Quite politely, he stated that he would have left too, but they were speaking from his wagon.

Yvonne Louise Pavy Weiss Bourgeois
Courtesy of Ida Pavy Boudreaux

Judge Benjamin Henry Pavy
Courtesy of Ida Pavy Boudreaux

Chapter II

Weiss Family Description

The Weiss family history in America began with Carl Thomas Weiss, grandfather of Carl Austin Weiss. He was a German musician who moved to New Orleans from Munich in 1870. He was one of six children and had been disowned by his father because he refused to support his country in the Franco-Prussian War. In New Orleans he worked at Holy Trinity Jesuit Church as an organist and choir director. He also taught in the Jesuit School, where his son Carl Adam Weiss studied. The son became a pharmacist but was "forced" by his father to study medicine. He graduated from Tulane MedicalSchool in 1900.

Dr. Carl Adam Weiss, the alleged assassin's father, practiced medicine on a plantation in Lobell, Louisiana. He married Viola Maine, who was of Irish and French heritage. Carl Austin Weiss (not Jr.) was born in Baton Rouge where the mother had temporarily moved in order to give birth in the city.

Dr. Carl A. Weiss, Jr. sent me the following history of his father.

Carl Austin Weiss, Sr. grew up at 535 N. Fifth St. in Baton Rouge, where his parents had moved from New Orleans. His father, Carl Adam Weiss, had been a pharmacist first, then a physician, and later specialized, such as it was then, in eye, ear, nose, and throat. I believe Carl Adam had a considerable influence on my father, as he followed his footsteps both in Medicine and in ENT and returned to practice with him in their shared office at the Reymond Building in downtown Baton Rouge. Carl Austin graduated from Catholic High

School in Baton Rouge and went on to college and medical school, finishing, I believe, at a rather young age of about 21. He learned German fluently from a relative other than his father, and French as well, from whom I don't know.

He went to Europe for a rather prolonged stay, earning a "Zeugnis" or "certificate" in ENT pathology in Vienna which was then in the forefront, and spent time at the American Hospital in Neuilly, an outskirt of Paris. I gather he was a house officer at the time, and it was a vibrant time to be in Europe. In a book Papa Doc, about Hemingway, reference is made to his having known my father. By co-incidence, Yvonne Pavy was in Paris at about that time, the late twenties, as a representative of Louisiana as it celebrated the sesquicentennial of the Acadian migration. They wore "period" clothing for a photograph taken of the group with Marechal Foch, a celebrated hero of WWI. Their shared experience in France was an uniting topic when they later met.

My father had played the piano well, so that his parents said that locking up the Steinway was the sternest reprimand they could offer. Tom Ed, incidentally, was about 10 years his junior, while his sister Olga was several years his junior. Carl Austin also enjoyed carving (a small bust he had carved survived to my youth) and somewhere along the line he came to enjoy fencing.

The residency in ENT at Bellevue in New York City was very desirable, and contained elements of plastic reconstruction since ENT men did face lifts then, as well as mastoid and sinus surgery, tonsils, adenoids, and some head and neck cancers. One of my father's notebooks outlined the methods they were taught, with considerable attention to local and regional anesthetics using primarily cocaine, which is an excellent local anesthetic and astringent. Another book that survived, and that I still enjoy, was a short summary of the books he read in French and in English, as well as marginal notes on the music he enjoyed. There were also architectural features such as arches and pediments that caught his fancy. The French he wrote was excellent, but I have never seen any German writing. He and my mother had discussed the house he planed to build, with the design to be largely his own.

He had been interested in electricity early on and managed to "steal" power from the electric line of the tram in Baton Rouge for the electrification of a "playhouse". He was early into radio and x-ray equipment, which I believe he assembled himself.

My mother barely knew him as they were married only a short while, perhaps two years after a short engagement, as was then the fashion. The wedding was held in St. Landry's Church in Opelousas in December of 1933, and I was born in June of 1935. As I mentioned, Ida confirms that she has never seen a photograph of the event. The reception took place at the house on Cherry Street. I think my father was much taken with the Pavy family, as my grandfather was then a County Judge and he knew Dr. Octave and Dr. Albert to be physicians. My father had profound reli-

gious convictions and was a devout Catholic.

My father had encountered Mussolini's "Blackshirts" in Rome. (He had stayed a while in a pension in Florence, which he described in his notes. I stayed there, too, in 1954 attempting to retrace some of his steps.) He felt threatened by them, recalling that they forced bystanders off the sidewalks as they passed. Politics in Vienna were stormy, too, but I don't have any knowledge of my father's reaction. As to Huey Long, Carl's feelings were overshadowed by those of his father, Carl Adam, who saw the changes in the community of Baton Rouge more clearly and reacted more forcefully. When she heard that Dr. Carl Weiss had been killed, I believe my grandmother's first fear was that it was her husband, and not her son.

My father enjoyed firearms, and had bought a Belgian Browning .32-cal. automatic pistol, used, in a shop in Paris, for $25, and reported it as an item on his papers upon entering the States. He was seen to carry it in NYC by his friends (specifically, Dr. John McCauley, a colleague who became a Professor of Orthopedics. John was my teacher, a most reflective man, who was the only one to speak of my father's voice as a clear memory of his) though I believe the Sullivan Law had been passed by then, making handgun ownership without a permit a felony in the city.

My father was about 5'10" or 5'11", and was slight at about 140-150 lbs. (perhaps even less) according to autopsy reports as I remember them. He had black hair, as does his brother Tom, and wore thick dark rimmed glasses. He was very myopic.

*My maternal grandfather's difficulties
with the Opelousas "Gerrymander" (so
named after a Boston politician, Eldridge
Gerry, who proposed a voting district in Mas-
sachusetts so convoluted that it was likened
to a mythical animal of his own design) were
known to my father, as was the dismissal of
Paul, D. Pavy of the Opelousas School system and Marie Aline Pavy, a young teacher
and his wife's dear sister. How keenly he felt
these injuries is pure conjecture.*

*The proximity of my parents' home on
Lakeland Drive to the state capitol bears mention, as does the fact that the route he traveled took him essentially through the capitol
grounds. The family had one car, a black Buick
that Carl Austin shared with Carl Adam, and
I don't know where it was to be returned that
night...whether to Lakeland Drive where they
had a very modest house, or to Fifth Street
which was not very far removed. I suspect it
would have been to Lakeland Drive and there
he would have picked his father up and driven
him to the Reymond Bldg. the next day.*

*Donald, I offer you these details as the
sum total of what I know of my father. Though
it seems sketchy to me, I suspect that some sons
know less, since the premature death that occurred does tend to "focus the mind". I might
add parenthetically that my father had a life
insurance policy with New England Life for
$5000 which paid my mother $18.75 per
month all the days of her life. It was his only
asset, and it was the subject of an objection
that Uncle Veazie dealt with as the carrier*

*denied "double indemnity" on the grounds
that my father had been "the cause of his own
death", suggesting a virtual suicide. This position did not prevail.*

Dr. Edgar Hull, one of Louisiana's most famous physicians, once Dean of LSU Medical School, and involved in
the treatment of Huey in his final hours, was valedictorian of
the 1927 Tulane Medical School class. Weiss was salutato-
rian. They were roommates and dear friends.

On the fateful Sunday, September 8, 1935, Dr. Weiss
and his wife attended early mass in Baton Rouge and had
dinner with the elder Dr. and Mrs. Weiss. They later all went
to a camp on the Amite River. The younger couple swam
while the elder couple tended to the baby who was a few
months old. They later motored back to the city. Dr. Weiss
bathed, called a colleague about an operation that was set for
the next morning, and left to visit a patient. He seemed in
good spirits and was in no way acting as if he had murder on
his mind. He was 29 years old and had a promising future.
On this day he seemed very carefree, giving absolutely no
hint that he could have even thought of murder.

I first met Dr. Tom Ed Weiss in 1947 when I was 16
years old. I was a patient at the old Ochsner Hospital in New
Orleans near the Mississippi River Bridge. I had suffered a
fracture of my neck. Tom Ed, a rheumatologist, visited me
often. While writing this book I spoke to him many times. He
related interesting stories about his brother.

Carl's best friend was Dr. John Archinard whom he
met while interning at Touro Hospital. Archinard was from
France and had a brother who did research with Louis Pas-
teur. John later became an internist in New Orleans. Archinard
taught Carl both French and fencing. They fenced without
protective tips on their swords. The explanation was that they
wanted to see who would "draw first blood." They were also
in Europe at the same time and vacationed together, traveling

across Europe.

Carl was known to play the clarinet, saxophone, organ, and piano. He often played the organ at the Little Sisters of the Poor Nursing Home near Tuoro. Dr. Rudolph Matas of New Orleans, a world renowned surgeon, taught and befriended Carl during his internship. Matas also secured his appointment to the American Hospital in Paris.

In Paris he studied under Dr. deMartel, a neurosurgeon. In those times, before antibiotics, brain infections often were associated with sinusitis and mastoiditis. Pathology of the brain, ear, nose, and throat was of special interest to him. Dr. deMartel could not live under German rule, so the day the Germans marched into Paris he committed suicide.

Carl was buried the day after the shooting. Huey Long was not yet dead. On the way home from the funeral Tom Ed stated that his mother said, "Now Carl is dead. Let us all pray that Senator Long lives." In discussion about Huey's life and character the worst Tom Ed would say was that Huey was a "nuisance." Later he opined that Huey "must be having a tough time in purgatory." This, I thought, was a perfect example of magnanimity, considering the loss he suffered and the untruths he endured for so long.

Only three words are needed to describe the Weiss family: intellectual, cultured, and charitable. Unfortunately, the Long faction has made the family known publicly as something quite different.

Dr. Carl Austin Weiss
Courtesy The Louisiana Collection,
State Library of Louisiana
Baton Rouge, Louisiana

Dr. Carl Adam Weiss
Courtsey of Dr. Tom Ed Weiss

Dr. Carl Austin Weiss, Jr. (retired orthopedic surgeon) and
Dr. Carl Austin Weiss III (general surgeon in academic medi-
cine with a doctorate in moleculer biology)
Courtesy of Ida Pavy Boudreaux

Chapter III

A Brother's Description

"The boast of heraldry, the pomp of pow'r,
And all that beauty, all that wealth e'er gave,
Awaits alike the inevitable hour:
The paths of glory lead but to the grave."
Gray's Elegy -1750

Huey Long was born and raised in Winn Parish in northeastern Louisiana. He was one of eleven children. The family was not as poor as Huey would have had people believe. One brother was a dentist in Oklahoma. Julius Long, the older brother, was a lawyer. Earl, a younger brother, was later an equally controversial governor.

Early in life Huey was a salesman and traveled extensively in North Louisiana and became acquainted with many people. He married Rose McConnell. Huey's first elected political position was on the Railroad Commission. He ran for governor twice, being victorious on his second attempt in 1927.

Huey later became a U.S. Senator and became known nationally. It was thought that he planned to challenge President Franklin Roosevelt in 1936 or 1940.

Many books and articles have been written about Huey Long, but the most revealing and interesting publication is by his older brother, Julius Long. This was published by <u>Real America</u> in September and October, 1933. This magazine is no longer in print.

These articles and other books reveal much of Huey's complex psychological make up. He had difficulty in his relations with his siblings and many former friends. Political allies became his enemies. He was often vicious when attacking his foes and seemed to relish demeaning everyone who was not on his side.

Julius sent a letter to ex-Lieutenant Governor Paul Cyr, who was denied office of governor in 1930 when Huey was elected to the U.S. Senate. Julius had hoped his articles would be widely read and would help to overthrow Huey. Cyr, a dentist, once an ally of Huey, became a bitter enemy. His family feared violence. His sons, Louis and Charles, armed with shotguns, often spent nights in trees guarding their home.

Julius loaned Huey money to attend Tulane Law School, which he attended for less than a year. He passed the bar and became a partner with Julius in Shreveport, Louisiana. Huey wrote a letter demanding Julius vacate the office and then dissolved the practice. They made up but later dissolved the practice for good. A few months later Julius represented Huey in a slander suit against Governor John M. Parker. Huey was fined one dollar and given a thirty day suspended jail sentence.

Earl Long, Huey's brother, worked tirelessly for Huey, supporting him for railroad commissioner and in the two races for governor. In 1931 Earl ran for lieutenant governor, at first with no objection from his governor brother. Later, Huey turned on him and supported Earl's opponent. Earlier, Julius and Earl had worked hard to line up the necessary fifteen senators to sign the famous "Round Robin," in which the senators agreed not to vote against Huey, regardless of the charges, when Huey was impeached by the House.

It was apparent in 1931 that Huey's siblings "divorced themselves from him," Julius writes in Real America. Julius wrote that Earl was cheated out of votes for Lt. Governor. The Long family was upset. Earl supported his aged father and sick sister for years. One sister publicly stated that Huey was a traitor to the family.

In Real America, Julius recalls that Harly B. Boseman was a close friend and classmate of Huey. He loaned Huey money and helped get Huey jobs. He posted bail to get Huey out of jail in Shreveport and once wired money to Huey in Memphis. When Huey became Governor, Boseman was

33

elected to the legislature. He headed the Tax Commission and helped Huey when he was impeached. Boseman resigned the Tax Commission. Huey then turned on him and became his enemy for no explainable reason.

In the 1928 election for governor, Huey courted and received the support of Colonel Robert Ewing, publisher of The New Orleans States, The Shreveport Times, The Monroe Morning World, and The Monroe Times-Star. Colonel John P. Sullivan, a prominent New Orleans attorney, also supported Huey. Julius wrote that later Huey "deliberately kicked them out." Huey was not able to find a pretext.

Julius believed Huey learned much of his oratorical style that had a judicial "tone and manner" from a John H. Moran. He made speeches with Huey in 1918 in Liberty Loan drives, who told of his heroic battles, experiences, and wounds in World War I. It turned out he had stolen the uniform and papers of a Canadian soldier by that name. He was later defended by Huey for passing hot checks, interdicted, and sent to an insane asylum as a result of Huey's pleadings.

Huey rarely went to church and Julius felt that Huey quoted the bible for political reasons. Julius denounced Huey for his "profanity and vulgarity." He claimed a defrocked preacher who ran off with the wife of a prominent man was often consulted for "scriptural quotations." Julius claims Huey later successfully used a Bible quotation in a political contest.

Julius said often Huey was drinking on a platform "slandering" others and surrounded by "gunmen." If any one of these gunmen would injure one of Huey's enemies they would not be punished in Louisiana. Julius wrote, "and if one of Huey's gunmen should kill a man who was resenting Huey's slanders, the murderer would never suffer for his deed; not in the State of Louisiana."

This, I feel, is an interesting observation and probably set the tone or mental state of Huey's bodyguards. They were being directed by their leader who had some paranoid tendencies with strained feelings towards his enemies.

Senator Huey P. Long
Courtesy Russell Billiu Long Papers, Mss. 3700, Louisiana
and Lower Mississippi Valley Collections, LSU Libraries,
Louisiana State University, Baton Rouge, Louisisna

Most recognize that Huey had a brilliant intellect, was cunning, and resourceful in political maneuvering. He turned friends into enemies, often for inexplicable reasons. Huey's deception was demonstrated by his activities before an election. He would hire people and send them to certain areas to tell the populace new roads would be built. He even had trees felled. People in these localities would vote for him. No roads were ever built.

I like the example of Huey finding himself up against a hostile legislature when he was first elected governor. He encouraged his allies to hurriedly pass all bills by the opposition and have more time to get his own bills passed. Later, he vetoed opposition bills. Huey did things like eat out of other peoples plates and scratch his buttocks. His great intellect, his antisocial activities at times, his control of others, his difficulty with maintaining certain personal relationships, and his prominence on the national scene should encourage study by some psychiatric departments. Huey Long was driven by his own ego. He appeared to have had a manic-depressive personality. Although many books have been written about Huey, so far nobody has done a psychological evaluation. More in depth study should be made of his very interesting psychic make-up. I think dominant people in history, such as Caesar and Napoleon, had a mental chemistry much like that of Huey Long.

Julius concludes that he wanted Huey retired from public office, as he was a humiliation to the Long family. Julius made the prophetic statement that the "more powerful Huey becomes, the greater will be the crash of his inevitable collapse."

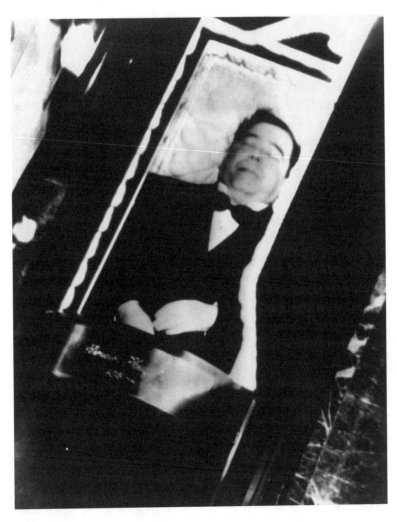

Senator Huey P., Long
Courtesy Russell Billiu Long Papers, Mss. 3700, Louisiana
and Lower Mississippi Valley Collections, LSU Libraries,
Louisiana State University, Baton Rouge, Louisiana

Chapter IV

The Pulse of The Times

For most people it is difficult to understand the temper of the times in 1935. There was polarization, animosity, and hatred between the Longs and the anti-Longs. Ida Pavy Boudreaux, sister of Yvonne Pavy Weiss, recalls, " In those days everyone was always classified as either pro-Long or anti-Long in almost any conversation among my family and close friends."

There were often confrontations. Long was egged and hung in effigy. Huey's bodyguards beat people and reporters. Some members of the legislature carried pistols. Representative George Perrault of Opelousas always had a pistol in his brief case. There were groups with arms and one such group in East Baton Rouge Parish planned to storm the state house but had second thoughts. They briefly held the courthouse .

As governor, Huey Long passed laws in special sessions to consolidate his power. He created commissions that would control local governmental bodies and officials, and did many vindictive and punitive things to his enemies.

In August 1934, in New Orleans, Governor Allen, generally considered Long's puppet, proclaimed partial martial law and the National Guard seized the voter registration office. The New Orleans police force and others numbering about 1,000 were called. Long called in 2,000 National Guardsmen. A machine guns face-off between the New Orleans Police Force and the National Guard lasted for days. Fortunately no fighting occurred.

On January 24, 1935, one hundred armed citizens met at the Baton Rouge Airport in response to a martial law declaration. State troopers and guardsmen, sent to storm the airport, advanced on the group which surrendered or ran. One gun was fired and a man was wounded. This was called "the Battle of the Airport."

A Long spy claimed his opponents planned to shoot Huey as his car passed in a curve near Baton Rouge.

On Sunday, July 21, and Monday, July 22, 1935, a meeting of Long opponents, all democrats, held a caucus in the DeSoto Hotel in New Orleans. The meeting was to plot against Huey in the next January election. Huey later claimed that there were plotters at the meeting who planned to kill him. The Senator drew national attention when he read a transcript in the US Senate on August 9, 1935, of a recording device placed in the meeting. One of the two men who certified the transcript was later convicted of perjury. Huey read that someone said he "would draw a lottery and go out and kill Huey Long. It would take one man, one gun, and one bullet." Further, he read, "sixty percent of the people want him in the Gulf of Mexico weighted with chains. The trouble is getting the various elements together." Then, "I haven't the slightest doubt that Roosevelt would pardon anyone who killed Long." Roosevelt became more and more alienated by Huey who made stinging, demeaning statements about the president. The Senator was involved in national politics and developed "Share The Wealth" clubs all over the country. Thousands wrote to him seeking his leadership.

After Huey's death, his people said there was, as noted on the tape, a "Dr. Wise" at the DeSoto Hotel meeting. Huey did not mention this name earlier on the Senate floor. Also there were rumors that straws were pulled and that "Dr. Wise" drew the short straw and was chosen to kill Huey. These accusations were nonsense. Weiss was in Opelousas on Sunday, the 21st and in his office all day on the 22nd. His records even show he treated a niece of Huey on that day. In the Louisiana State Archives is a list of all those registered at the DeSoto Hotel. This was obtained by the Bureau of Criminal Investigation. No Pavy or Weiss was found to have registered at the Desoto.

In an affidavit dated March 31, 1999, Alfred Smith
Landry, a well-respected New Iberia attorney, stated:

> I am a lifelong resident of Iberia Parish, Loui-
> siana, having practiced law in this Parish for
> over 47 years.
>
> I was friendly with a man named Rob-
> ert B. LeBlanc who owned the ford dealership
> in New Iberia. Bob had a houseboat which he
> kept at Avery Island, powered by a couple of
> outboard motors, and it was his practice to
> take the houseboat out on Sunday morning
> with a group of his friends and to fish for
> croakers, speckled trout, and other saltwater
> species in the inland bayous and canals be-
> tween Avery Island and Vermilion Bay.
>
> On one of those Sundays I was on Bob's boat,
> fishing with him, with a man named Warren
> Jefferson and possibly with others whose
> names I do not remember. Both Bob and War-
> ren were older than I was by about 30 years,
> but I had utmost respect for both of them.
>
> Mr. Jefferson was a grandson of the
> great actor of his time, Joe Jefferson, after
> whom Jefferson Island is named and who
> owned the "Island" at one time. The story goes
> that as a young man Warren Jefferson was a
> hell-raiser and that he was sent down to Loui-
> siana from Massachusetts to work and settle
> down. Mr. Jefferson met and married a Cajun
> girl and lived here for the rest of his life, fa-
> thering two sons, Joseph W. Jefferson and
> Charles B. Jefferson. Mr. Jefferson owned and
> operated a business called Jefferson Insurance
> Agency.

Although Mr. Jefferson was not wealthy, he was a man of unquestioned character and reputation in this community, a person for whom everybody had a lot of respect.

The Sunday of my conversation with Mr. Jefferson took place about 25 or 30 years ago, and as I was fishing with Mr. Jefferson, from the top deck of the houseboat, I mentioned to him the fact that I was reading one of the Huey Long books and that Mr. Jefferson was named in the book as having been present at the infamous meeting in the DeSota Hotel in New Orleans, at which members of the anti-Long forces were said to have plotted to have Huey Long killed. I asked him if that was true. His reply, as well as I can remember is, was this:

"Yes, I was there, and there was a meeting of anti-Long people in the DeSota Hotel, as reported but although somebody may have said, 'we ought to kill the son-of-a-bitch', no plan to kill Huey Long was discussed or made at that meeting." And then he added:

"But there was a meeting that took place around that time in Plaquemine, and I believe that your father was there, and two hired killers from Texas came to that meeting and offered to dispose of Long for $10,000.00, but they wanted all of the money in advance. The group would not agree to payment of the full amount in advance. The men from Texas left and the deal was never made."

Perhaps this will give some idea of the hard feeling and animosity which otherwise respectable, law-abiding, peace-loving men felt toward Huey Long, and the desperate measures they were willing to take to rid this state of him. There must have been very good cause for such men to feel that way.

Alfred Smith Landry

There probably were many people and groups wanting to do away with Huey and conspiracies may have been in the works. According to my interviews, one man from Bunkie, a relative of an Opelousas attorney, was "hell bent" on an assassination attempt.

The Morning Advocate reported on Monday the 9th of September, 1935: "Since Long has begun to tighten his dictatorial powers on the state, crushing his political enemies, there has been free talk of his assassination." Huey charged there had been several plots against him and, of late, he appeared to suffer from nerves. "Saturday night he was particularly wrought up and had an altercation with Thomas O. Harris, former newspaper man and publicity director of the federal educational department. One of the bodyguards struck Harris in the face after the verbal row and then Senator Long stormed about the capitol, shaking his finger at newsmen and others." It should be noted that Thomas Harris was the author of a biography on Huey Long.

Dr. Thomas Weiss had an interview with Senator Russell Long some years after the shooting. Tom asked why Huey always had bodyguards. The son's answer was that his father had a great fear of being shot. His bodyguards always told Huey that it was possible that someone could indeed get through them and shoot him. They, however, assured and pledged to him that this person or persons would be immediately shot to death. In almost all gatherings of anti-Longs the shooting or killing of Long was frequently a part of the conversation. Long, of course, invited much of the antagonism against him by his vindictiveness, but this certainly fed on his fears. These fears were imparted to his bodyguards. They no doubt were every moment ready to pounce on anyone who would be a threat to their leader. Shoot first and ask questions later is exactly what I believe happened that night of September 8, 1935, at 9:22 p.m. Guns were holstered, but brains were cocked.

Chapter V

Shakespeare in Louisiana

If, indeed, Dr. Weiss had no gun, and he and Huey were shot by Huey's bodyguards, then the entire cover-up was a masterful theatrical performance. The martyrdom of Huey Long has been believed by many for years. Each "eye witness" had a part to play. It was well directed. Some often joked that it took an entire week to teach the witnesses their lines. I will allow the reader to decide who wins an Oscar!

For the most part, all eyewitnesses seemed to agree generally with what happened that fateful night of September 8, 1935. There are, however, some discrepancies. For years, the only official records were the death certificates of Dr. Weiss and Senator Long. The newspaper accounts until 1985 are the only sources of information for the inquest conducted by District Attorney John Fred Odom. The inquest was held September 16. Twenty-one witnesses testified in a two and a half hour period. Of significance is that not one person at the scene was anti-Long. I have been given a copy of District Attorney Odom's inquest with a letter that helps to explain what happened to this document. The document was "lost" until placed in the Congressional Record by Senator Russell Long on September 10, 1985.

Dracus Burke, who spent his career as a prosecutor in the Air Force, and later as an Assistant District Attorney in the Iberia Parish area, evaluated the inquiry. He wrote: "The paramount impression I get from this transcript is one of appalling incompetence and lack of professionalism in the Governor's bodyguard." He further noted: "This coroner's inquest was incredibly superficial considering the prominence of the victim." He normally notices discrepancies in testimony of witnesses and suspects a cover up when all witnesses agree. In recent times extensive investigations have been done in cases where citizens have been shot or abused by police.

Dr. Billy Cook was the surgeon who operated on Huey following the shooting. He was held in great respect by the nurses I interviewed. He was questioned only about Huey's lip. Attorney General Gaston Porterie, who observed the hearing, asked Dr. Cook if this wound could have been caused by a fall. Here District Attorney Odom had a great chance to acquire details of the surgery. He asked no questions. I am led to believe that Odom and Porterie agreed in advance not to inquire about the surgery. There seem to have been ground rules and boundaries set by these two men. Porterie, 100% pro-Long, could have had an inquiry and report of his own. It would have been much better for his law school classmate and long time friend, Odom, anti-Long, to have directed the investigation.

The following is a summary of sources as to events of September 8, 1935: Senator Long walked into the Governor's office after walking down the corridor. He came out of the office into the corridor, which is about twelve feet wide. Many people were in this small area. Dr. Weiss, without saying a word, allegedly came up to Huey with a small gun. John Fournet, former Speaker of the House and later Chief Justice of Louisiana Supreme Court, said he saw this and was able to hit the gun so it was fired into Huey's abdomen instead of his chest. Bodyguard Murphy Roden held the gun and hand of Weiss, pulling his own gun some way and apparently was first to shoot Weiss. Bodyguard Elliot Coleman swung twice at Weiss, missed and then hit Weiss in the face. He then shot him. This is important because he is the first and only person to admit to fisticuffs. Bodyguards Paul Votier and Joe Messina also fired at Weiss. Votier claims that Coleman hit Weiss with his fist but missed in his first attempt and may have hit Long when missing Weiss. There were 61 bullet holes in the doctor's body, so over 30 bullets were fired. Coleman always denied that he hit Huey on the lip.

Huey ran down the corridor, went down the stairs and was met first by Public Service Commissioner Jimmy

O'Conner in the basement. Huey told him he was shot and spit blood on him. O'Conner then thought that he was shot in the mouth. Bodyguard Joe Vitrano, in an interview with Ed Reed, author of *Requiem For A Kingfish*, stated he followed Huey down the stairs. Vitrano claims Huey slipped, hit the wall and cut his lip when he was at the bottom of the steps. Vitrano did not testify in the inquiry. Jimmy O'Conner saw Huey coming down the steps and did not record that he fell. Most accounts claim Huey left the scene immediately after being shot. The shooting occurred at 9:22 p.m. but this time has been debated by some.

There are several significant differences in the testimony of witnesses. First, some thought there was one shot followed by many after a pause. Others seem to believe there was a shot, followed by a pause, a second shot and a pause before the many shots. C. A. Riddle, a state representative from Avoyelles Parish, saw the shooting but claims he was five to six feet from Long and did not see Fournet, who was supposed to be standing next to Long. I feel this has significance because the statement that he didn't see Fournet conflicts with Fournet's own statement that he (Fournet) was standing next to Huey and heroically hit the gun away from Huey's heart. Riddle also stated that Weiss was five to six feet away from Huey. This was a glaring contradiction of other witnesses.

Rev. Gerald K. Smith, involved in Huey's "Share the Wealth" program, refused to make a statement at the inquiry. He stated that Odom was "one of the co-plotters of this assassination." Odom countered with the statement that Smith was "a willful, vicious, and deliberate liar."

This confrontation enhanced Odom's position as anti-Long, exactly what the Long faction wanted. No contempt citation was executed.

Bodyguard George McQuiston stated, "I don't care to make any statements whatsoever." Nothing was done to force a statement. McQuiston was illiterate and he probably feared speaking in public. The Long regime probably had concerns about his ability to field any questions. McQuiston had a sister, Billy Joe, who was executed in Lake Charles in the early 1940's. She had shot a man in cold blood but professed to be a devout Catholic while in prison. Her case was well known at the time and efforts were made to save her from execution.

Michael Wynne, Long authority and collector of memorabilia has McQuiston's small caliber revolver which McQuiston carried in a leg holster. To his knowledge, no other bodyguards' revolvers have been found that have been documented.

My conclusion is that this was a brief, pathetic hearing and not a trial. It was based on circumstantial assumptions of motives, with no direct evidence of intent. Witnesses were obviously biased and made self-serving statements without any cross-examination. No physical evidence was presented to support a finding of guilt.

This hearing was a sounding board for the assassination deception. It served the Long Regime very well. No conclusions were reached or statements made by District Attorney Odem. From this hearing the so-called "Official Version" was formed and became the "Official History".

Associated Press reporter Desobry was the first to release the news to the world. His comments give a picture of the mad scene and attitude of the guards. David Zinman in his book, *The Day Huey Long Was Shot,* almost brings the happenings to life in his description.

"In the Governor's corridor, the reporters saw plainclothesmen brandishing pistols and machine guns pulled from their hiding places and set up." Desobry picked out the biggest crowd and fought his way into it. "You could almost hear the feeling of hate and passion all about," Desobry said. "The grim faces looked murderous." Despite shoving by bodyguards, he managed to push to the front. There was the doctor's body. It was a sight he would never forget.

"Against the background of the white suit, I could see in bold relief, the scores of bullets that had punctured his body," Desobry said. "His body looked like a punchboard with all the numbers out. I went close, leaned down, and looked at him, not to see if he was dead because there could be no doubt of that, but to see if I knew him. He was a stranger."

All this happened in a matter of seconds. Desobry grasped one person after another trying to pick up pieces of the story.

"What happened?"

"He shot Huey."

The guards looked menacingly at reporters.

"They did it," one fellow shouted hysterically. "They caused all this! Those damn reporters."

"Shoot 'em all," shrilled another."

Other reporters stated that the bodyguards almost shot someone else.

One reporter, E. Frampton , who gave testimony at the District Attorney's inquest, stated he heard a shot as he was opening the door into the corridor from the governor's office. He opened the door and saw Weiss being shot and Huey walking away. Frampton was a reporter with The New Orleans Item but was also on the state payroll and considered pro-Long. He did give an eyewitness account the next day in The New Orleans Item. Twenty years later, Frampton told author Zinman that he actually saw Weiss shoot Senator Long. This contradicts his earlier testimony and when this was pointed out he said "he would go by what he said in 1935," (*The Day Huey Long Was Shot*, by David Zinman, pp.266-267).

The bodyguards were committed to protect Huey always with trigger finger at the ready. This was mentally infused into them by Huey who was constantly in fear of being shot. They could easily panic and shoot almost anyone if some incident would develop. This, I believe, set the stage

47

for the actual happenings of Sepember 8, 1935.

Of great interest is the $20,000.00 life insurance policy on Huey Long. The Mutual Insurance Company of New York (MONY) paid double indemnity to the Long family based on an extensive investigation conducted by its own investigator, K.B. Ponder. The payment would have been made if death was caused by accident or murder. Author Zinman was able to obtain this extensive report of November 11, 1936. Some facts are not correct but it is obviously from an objective source from outside Louisiana.

This report is directed to H.P. Gallaher, Superintendent, Bureau of Investigation, New York, NY. The opening paragraph is as follows:

> *In connection with the above-mentioned instructions, I submit the following report. The information contained herein has been obtained from various sources, is considered reliable, and I believe represents the true background, causes and facts surrounding the death of the insured. For reasons which will be fully explained in the report, some of the circumstances herein set out cannot be proved, for to prove anything in connection with the life and death of the insured would necessitate involving people associated with the insured in his political and personal life. Naturally there have been any number of rumors in connection with this case, documentary evidence has been destroyed, or else it was set up in the beginning to represent conditions in the light most favorable to the insured and to those who expected to profit most by the political control the insured had established over the State of Louisiana.*

He concludes by writing:

Long was buried on the grounds of the new State Capitol Building. He is buried deep, with tons of concrete in the underground vault. His political friends said that this was done to insure that he would never be moved. Others said that it was done so that none might ever have a chance to examine the body.

There is no doubt that his death was accidental, but the consensus of more informed opinion is that he was killed by his own guard and not by Weiss.

Yours very truly,
K.B. Ponder

Death Certificate of Senator Huey P. Long
Courtesy of Louisiana Department of State, Division of Archives,
Records Management and History

Death Certificate of Dr. Carl A. Weiss
Courtesy of Louisiana Department of State, Division of Archives,
Records Management and History

Chapter VI

The Hospital

O'Conner rode to the hospital with Huey. There is limited information as to what happened. The Long family has always stood by the "official version" of witnesses. There is no evidence that x-rays were taken. Dr. Arthur Vidrine was the surgeon history records who treated and operated on Huey. Dr. Vidrine, a physician from Eunice, was appointed both Administrator of New Orleans Charity Hospital and Dean of the LSU Medical School, and happened to be in Baton Rouge at the time of the shooting. There was bitterness between Vidrine and some of the New Orleans physicians. Huey had requested Dr. Urban Maes, Chief of Surgery at LSU Medical School in New Orleans, to operate. Maes and Dr. James Rives were involved in an auto mishap on the way to Baton Rouge from New Orleans, and were delayed in arrival. New Orleans surgeon Dr. Russell Stone was called, but arrived later. Dr. Edgar Hull, a brilliant young resident in internal medicine, was also brought into the case from New Orleans. A number of other M.D.s were called into the case. Vidrine is credited with being the doctor in charge.

Dr. William Cook, a trained surgeon, was early on the scene and obviously consulted with Dr. Vidrine before surgery. Dr. Cecile Lorio, a pediatrician, was also in the case early as was his brother Dr. Clarence Lorio, another surgeon who arrived during the surgery. Dr. Henry McKown, staunch anti-Long, who had once said Huey would never awaken if he was called to put him to sleep, was indeed the anesthesiologist. He was actually a dentist. The general belief has been that Huey had an injury to the kidney, which was not addressed by the doctors. There is a brief description of the operation, which revealed the colon was perforated in two places. There was some bleeding noticed in the mesentery (the attachment of the intestine to the back wall). Huey died thirty hours after being shot. Four transfusions were given and a fever was observed.

In a personal interview with the scrub nurse, Melinda Delage, I learned that Dr. Vidrine was not the surgeon. She was very definite that Dr. Cook made the incision and Dr. Clarence Lorio arrived and replaced Dr. Cook as the surgeon. Dr. Cook, she recalls, grimaced at her. Dr. Joseph Sabatier, a medical student in the operating room, is not in complete accord with Mrs. Delage on this point. Also, the mortician stated the incision was made by Dr. Cook. Further, Dr. Cook was the only doctor called to the inquiry by District Attorney Odom.

Mrs. Delage also stated she did not actually observe a bullet wound of the abdomen but was busy with her duties and could have overlooked it.

The operation was almost like a sporting event with the operating room full of politicians.

In a 1971 edition of Louisiana Historical Quarterly, Dr. Loria (the LSU surgery professor) produced a copy of the one and only bulletin issued by Dr. Vidrine on September 9 at 5:15 a.m. He wrote, "Senator Long was shot through the right upper quadrant of the abdomen, the bullet going through the body. There were two penetrations of the transverse colon and considerable hemorrhage from the mesentery and omentum. The patient's condition is satisfactory and no important information will be available for 12 hours." (Note that often the transverse colon is high in the abdomen, and near the rib cage and sternum). This bulletin was approved by the politicians and cosigned by Huey's secretary, Earle Christenberry, Jr.

Dr. Frank Loria's account of the surgery was in the December 1948 issue of the International Abstracts of Surgeons. There, he stated very little blood was found in the abdominal cavity. Also in the account, he emphasizes by quotation that 'small' holes were in the colon and little soiling, with very little blood.

Dr. Russell Stone, a LSU surgery professor, told the New Orleans Times Picayune reporter, Edward F. Hebert (later elected to congress), that he was consulted after surgery. It was said that Dr. Vidrine had not checked the kidney and that Huey died from a hemorrhage. After consulting with Stone, Vidrine offered for Dr. Stone to operate. His well-quoted remark was, "I don't kill living patients." It is worthy of note that Dr. Stone and Dr. Vidrine were probably antagonists before September 1935. In 1935, a bullet wound of the abdomen was most often fatal due to development of peritonitis. Later survival improved with the advent of antibiotics. The historical opinion that Vidrine was blamed for errors probably started with Dr. Stone. I found no other public criticism by other physicians.

Dr. Stone was a proponent of the so-called buttonhole incision which implied, in those days, the smaller the incision the more talented the surgeon. Opponents of this felt that adequate exposure was a better surgical principle, especially in the days before antibiotics. New state-of-the-art technology, of course, changed these concepts since "buttonhole" surgery is now the "state-of-the-art." Dr. Stone, ironically, died of a ruptured appendix.

Our Lady of the Lake
Sanitarium
Baton Rouge, La.

Sept, 9th, 1935
5:15 am.

Senator Long was shot through the right upper quadrant of the abdomen, the bullet going through the body.

There were two penetrations of the transverse colon and considerable hemorrhage from the mesentery and omentum

The patient's condition is satisfactory and no important information will be available for about 72 hours.

Dr. Arthur Vidrine
Surgeon in Charge
By: Earle Christenberry
Secty. to Sen. Long

This is the one and only medical bulletin issued. It appears to have been written by Earle Christenberry, secretary to Huey Long. He signs Vidrine's name and designates him "Surgeon in Charge". This makes Vidrine the most responsible doctor on the case, and strongly suggests that political forces were involved in this medical case.

The Louisiana Collection, State Library of Louisiana; Baton Rouge, Louisiana

Chapter VII

Doctors

During Huey's day, there was considerable animosity among doctors in New Orleans because of politics. Tulane had refused Huey an honorary degree and some felt his efforts to expand LSU were motivated by this. Nevertheless, there was jealousy and animosity brewing. This is important to understand because Dr. Vidrine must have known Dr. Stone would be adversarial before the consultation after surgery. It is my feeling that Dr. Vidrine did not take Stone into his confidence. Here a small town doctor was propelled into prominence by political decree. He faced an eminent, metropolitan surgeon.

Dr. Alton Ochsner's position on the staff of Charity Hospital was threatened because of his opposition to Huey. Dr. Ochsner, chief of Tulane Surgery, and very anti-Long, was actually denied Charity Hospital privileges by Huey when Huey read a very critical letter written by Ochsner sent to someone in Baltimore. This letter was thought to have been stolen from Ochsner's dress clothes while he was in surgery.

The Accreditation Committee of the Association of Southern Universities threatened to deny LSU Medical School an "A" rating for this action by the governor, and also demanded an upgrading of the surgery department. A distinguished physician, Dr. Urban Maes, was appointed head of the surgery department. He accepted with the condition that Dr. Ochsner's privileges be restored, and that the governor would no longer interfere with the school or hospital. Huey was forced to suppress his vindictiveness, and Ochsner, through the hospital board which Huey controlled, was restored to the staff after a two-year hiatus.

There were many things that influenced the doctors in this case. The first consideration is the influence of Hippocrates, a Greek, who lived over 300 years before Christ.

He wrote the "Oath of Hippocratic," which physicians have sworn to for centuries. Certain selections of this oath are as follows. "I will follow that method of treatment which, according to my ability and judgment, I consider for the benefit of the patients, and abstain from whatever is deleterious and mischievous... With purity and holiness, I will pass my life and practice my art." "Whatever, in the connection of my professional practice, or not in connection with it, I may see or hear in the lives of men which ought not to be spoken aloud, I will not divulge, as recognizing that all such should be kept secret."

Doctors have always held that the doctor-patient relationship is a private one and is privileged. Any violation would be a serious breach of ethics. Also, it is clearly implied and respected in contract law in Louisiana. Further, the knowledge can not be violated by a court in civil cases. At present it cannot be violated, but in 1928, the law had never been challenged.

The physicians involved in Huey's case were obliged for ethical, moral and legal reasons not to divulge information of the case without the patient's or the family's consent. Now, bring to bear the powerful political forces that actually moved into the medical care. For example, Huey's trusted friend and power broker, Seymor Weiss (no relation to Carl), appeared to have some control of the operation and planned the funeral completely. To the credit of the doctors, none wrote any statements about the case. To do so would have been to either reveal facts or distort the truth.

It was great political good fortune for the Long faction that Huey would become a martyr and his followers would defeat the "assassination ticket" in the election in four months. All things seemed to have worked well in spite of the loss of the Kingfish. There was "one man, one gun, and one bullet." Will history correctly record what man, what gun, and what bullet?

Chapter VIII

A Class Reunion

For Homecoming each year Tulane Medical School holds medical lectures or brief programs. My 30th class reunion was in 1984 and the program was amazing to me because of the subject and the speakers. Huey Long's medical case and death were discussed. Dr. Frank Loria (no relation to the Baton Rouge Lorios) published a paper on penetrating wounds in a surgical journal in 1948. As a Professor of Surgery at LSU he studied Huey's case and tried to obtain information about the case. Dr. Loria interviewed some of the doctors and sent a questionnaire. In spite of the fact that Loria published his findings in a medical publication, his sources of information were, at best, limited. He reported in one article that there was one bullet hole in the right upper quadrant of the abdomen and another in the back side below the ribs not far from the spine, "The inner side of the mid scapular line." Dr. Loria's conclusion was that Huey died from a hemorrhage of the kidney.

Next to address the program was Dr. Edgar Hull, who was on the scene after the surgery. He was adamant and repeatedly stated that Huey did not die from hemorrhaging, but from peritonitis. Dr. Hull, in a wheelchair, weeks from his death, was feisty and even spoke out after the moderator closed the program. His argument was that he was with Dr. Jordan Kahle, the urologist, who drew no blood from a needle placed in the perinephric space (the area around the kidney). This schism of medical opinion by the very prominent physicians is typical of the many contradictory statements connected to the Long shooting, medical or otherwise.

The alumni were further treated to comments from Dr. Tom Ed Weiss, a rheumatologist at Oschner Clinic and brother of Carl Weiss. Weiss has always held that he was in college at LSU at the time of the shooting. He had found

Carl's car in the front of the capitol. It was obvious it had been opened and tampered with. The details of this matter will be addressed later.

Further, Dr. Tom Weiss offered the possibility that Huey was involved with the underworld and had, as was often his way, antagonized those in the underworld or broken off agreements. He offered the possibility that Huey was ultimately shot by his bodyguards acting as paid Mafia agents. His brother, he said, was a "pigeon." This view is probably held by some.

Last on the panel discussion was Judge Cecil Morgan who spoke of his dealings with Huey. He believed that antagonism toward Huey had reached such a fever pitch that it was only a matter of time before someone would kill him. "It just had to happen." Many of Judge Morgan's acquaintances said this. Morgan spoke eloquently that day and at great length.

My feeling is that I have to respect the call by Dr. Hull. He was there in 1935, on the scene. He was known as a "doctor's doctor," a very devout, religious man, and he knew he was living his last days. Dr. Hull was always recognized as a diagnostician with few peers. I would think that most, if not all, of the physicians trained by Dr. Hull would agree with his diagnostics. One problem here, however, is that a urologist indicated that a patient can bleed from the kidney and a negative aspiration still be possible.

Chapter IX

The Whitewashed Lip

Of all the happenings in the shooting of Senator Huey Long, an acknowledged fact was that Huey had a laceration or a bloodied lip. None contest this. Jewel O'Neal, a twenty-year-old student nurse, was in the presence of Huey and Dr. Vidrine when the doctor was cleaning Huey's wounds. The two were discussing the shooting and Vidrine asked about the laceration of the lip. The nurse noted this and handed Dr. Vidrine a towel. Huey simply stated, "That's where he hit me." Three months later she swore in a notarized statement that this was the truth. (This was reprinted on page 144 of *The Day Huey Long Was Shot*, by David Zinman.

In *Requiem for a Kingfish* Ed Reed interviewed Melinda Delage. He reported, "I interviewed the scrub nurse at Huey's operation and she told me that when asked by the anesthesiologist, "What happened to your lip?" Long replied, "That's where he hit me." I asked her who Huey was referring to. She replied, "Dr. Weiss."

In a personal interview with me, Mrs. Melinda Delage stated that she was in the operating room when Long was wheeled in on a stretcher. He seemed a bit quiet, as if sedated for surgery and/or very wounded. She was the scrub nurse and next to Dr. Cook, who actually made the incision and did the surgery until Dr. Clarence Lorio entered the case. Dr. Lorio then completed the surgery. She is very emphatic that Dr. Vidrine was not the surgeon and at the most was an assistant who contributed little to the operation.

Mrs. Delage is very certain she heard a conversation between Dr. McKowen, the anesthesiologist, and Senator Long. When questioned by the doctor about the lip injury, Huey rather gruffly stated, "That was where he hit me," apparently meaning Dr. Weiss. She emphasized that her recall of this is as though it had just happened. She stated that the left lower lip was involved and dried blood was on this area.

At first, Mrs. Delage was reluctant to talk to me and said she had nothing to say. With apparent fear and apprehension she stated she did not want to be shot. She related, later, that several years ago a man had called and threatened her. He warned her not to discuss the events in the operating room because she was wrong. She asked the man if he had been there. The elder Dr. Weiss asked her to testify about the lip if a possible suit was filed. Weiss later told her he had reconsidered, and to her remembrance, Dr. Weiss had feared he or Mrs. Delage would be put in danger.

The following is Mrs. Delage's letter written in January 1998:

> *It was the evening of September 8th, 1935 that Senator Long was shot, and was admitted to Our Lady of the Lake Hospital for surgery. I was a student nurse at that time. It was routine for the nurses who had completed their term in the surgery unit to take emergency calls. Jewel O'Neal acted in the capacity of circulating nurse, and I as scrub nurse. More than an hour elapsed before surgery was begun, (while waiting for Dr. Vidrine or Dr. Clarence Lorio.)*
>
> *Senator Long was brought into the operating room by stretcher. He was awake and appeared calm except moaning occasionally. While Dr. McKowen was preparing for the anesthesia, he noticed that the patient had a lacerated and swollen lip. He stepped from the head of the stretcher to the side and faced the patient and asked, "What is that on your lip?" and the patient answered, "Oh, that's where he hit me."*

Shortly after the anesthetic was begun, Dr. McKowen said to a doctor who was standing close by, "someone better hold his hand, because I don't want to be responsible it anything happens."

Dr. William Cook performed the surgery. Dr. Vidrine assisted. When the surgery was nearly completed, Dr. Clarence Lorio relieved Dr. Cook as surgeon, and Cook stepped aside. Surgery was completed. I did not observe a foreign body.

Melinda Bandiera DeLage

After the shooting Huey ran into the corridor of the capitol, then down the stairs to the basement. Before publishing his book in 1986, Ed Reed interviewed bodyguard Joe Vitrano. Vitrano claims to have followed behind Huey, down the staircase, and relates that Huey slipped on the last of the stairs, hit the wall, and split his lip.

The most important account of the lip injury was given by Jimmy O'Conner. He claimed he met Huey at the bottom of the stairs (Vitrano's account had Huey falling down the last of the stairs) and Huey was already bleeding from the lip. Huey told him he had been shot. Huey spit a significant amount of blood on O'Conner, leading O'Conner to believe, at first, that Huey had been shot in the mouth.

Associated Press reporter Desobry was on the scene shortly after the shooting. He viewed Weiss' body and noted that none of the bodyguards would talk about the shooting. Initially, only Huey could speak publicly.

All eyewitness accounts, reported by hallway observers, were that Weiss said or did nothing except walk up to Huey and shoot him. Judge Fournet claimed there was a fever blister on Huey's lip, a strange reason for the amount of bleeding reported, especially by O'Conner. The first coat of whitewash by the Long faction is that Weiss said or did nothing except come forward and shoot Huey. Two hospital nurses O'Neal and Delage, revealed that Weiss hit Huey on the lip. No one ever denied that there was a laceration or "fever blister." Now comes the second coat of whitewash. Professor T. Harry Williams stated that O'Conner noted a "fleck" of blood on Huey's lip. To begin with, the tilt to Huey's martyrdom by Williams was stated by some that the Long family had contributed money indirectly for bringing Williams' book to fruition. This "fleck" statement would seem to be very poor reporting of an historical fact. In one account O'Conner said blood "gushed" from Huey's lip. Too many people noted and commented on the bleeding lip. Could Williams have deliberately misconstrued this important fact? Further, Williams states authoritatively that Weiss did shoot Huey and that was that. His account of this whitewash helped to support the assassination belief.

Williams further states in his book that the idea that Weiss was not the assassin was a myth. In light of information now available, Williams is drawing criticism. Few can believe that Weiss, having hit Huey on the lip, was the assassin. There were a number of minor discrepancies in accounts of the shooting such as who fired the second shot, if Weiss fired twice, or had his gun jammed. Bodyguard Roden's watch was shot off by Weiss' second shot, or by a bullet fired by Elliot Coleman. Which one? This same Elliot Coleman swung at Weiss missing the first time and knocking him to the floor the second time. Then Coleman shot Weiss and Coleman, not Weiss, conceivably fired the second shot. Why did Elliot Coleman not shoot Weiss immediately? Were there fisticuffs before the shooting began? These events are of less importance than the fact that there was no discrepancy in the report that Weiss shot and did not hit Huey. What is peculiar is that witnesses gave testimony about seeing the shooting by Weiss. In the confined area of the shooting some should have stated, it would seem, that they were not in a position to all see clearly. Any slight deviation of their statement here would weaken the conspiracy. They all had to agree that Weiss said nothing and only shot. No fisticuffs by Weiss could be reported! The opposite is what Long told the doctors that, indeed, he was hit on the lip.

In *The Huey Long Murder Case,* Herman Deutch makes a very profound observation that Weiss could not have hit Huey on the lip and had time to pull out a gun, and then shoot him also! Getting more ridiculous would be that Weiss hit Huey on the lip (even with a gun) and then shot him. How about the possibility of Weiss shooting Huey and then hitting him on the lip? Most absurd would be the scenario of Weiss slugging Huey with one hand and shooting him with the other. Whom should we believe, the nurses or the bodyguards? Who had motive to "whitewash" the shooting account?

Chapter X

A Pulitzer Criticism

One important man of the Long Era who was bright and articulate was Cecil Morgan. Less known today, he was a major opponent of Huey in the legislature. He led the "Dynamite Squad" that did pass impeachment proceedings in the state House of Representatives. He was a native of Shreveport and became a judge in north Louisiana. He then had an illustrious career as one of the leading attorneys for Standard Oil in New Jersey. On his retirement, he became Dean of the Tulane Law School.

I had the great pleasure of meeting him twice. The second meeting was in his home in New Orleans. He was in his 90's at the time and very alert. A more charming and interesting gentleman one could never find. He always stated, "I do not know who shot Huey Long."

His son, Dr. Cecil Morgan, Jr., a physician in Birmingham, Alabama, sent me Judge Morgan's letter to Professor Wiley of Emory University History Department. This letter is a critique of Professor Williams' Pulitzer Prize winning book. A similar critique by Judge Morgan was printed in the Tulane Law Review. Anyone interested in the Long Era should read this article also.

Cecil Morgan
1435 Jackson Ave.
New Orleans, LA 70130
May 9,1970

Professor Bell I. Wiley
Department of History
Emory University
Atlanta, Georgia 30322

Dear Professor Wiley:

This is an attempt to give you something of an answer to your December 1969 inquiry about the T. Harry Williams book on Huey Long. This is not a definitive appraisal, but is a beginning. I have read the book carefully, all 884 pages of it, and have made some marginal notes, and am trying to adjust my thinking to the formulation of a balanced estimate of his work. To begin with, you must understand that I was partisan, and associated with very strong minded people who opposed Huey Long, and we lived through some very trying times.

Consequently, I am inclined to greater caution now in retrospect, regarding what I say, than I exercised in the midst of a rough fight. But nonetheless, in retrospect, and with due caution, and with forty years added to my maturity, my only regret has to do with my inexperience and naivete, a kind of naivete that was not, as some have said—that I was "used" by the politicians, but rather that I was unaware of some of the social forces motivating various groups. I do not mind being "used" for my own purposes. As to the positions I took, the fight we waged and our estimate of what was right and wrong about the issues remain the same.

In recent times I have reviewed the record of the impeachment in 1929, and am more than ever convinced of the validity of the charges. I have watched the political evolution of the state, and as the old alignments of Long and Anti-Long forces fade, and new alignments emerge, I am more than ever con-

vinced that the impact of Longism was so great and its degrading influence so powerful that the political moral level to which the state sank during that regime is still exceedingly low, and lack of public confidence in elected officials makes decent government much more difficult. I will make these observations about the book as I see it now.

Professor Williams did a prodigious job of research. He has reported the positions taken by the opposing forces. They were from the press and are a matter of factual history. He has done this very well, and I think he has written a readable book, and that it is a contribution to the literature, and I am pleased that he received the Pulitzer Prize.

But he reports he has had access to Long family and friend sources not available to others, and was the direct or indirect beneficiary of Russell Long's bounty, and has written a work, we understand, the Long family approve of, and while he interviewed many people, including me, he failed to interview any number of other Anti-Long people who had a wealth of information, and strong feelings on the Anti-Long side. Among those not interviewed, who should have been, is Hodding Carter, who while not on the scene at the time of the impeachment, was there for the scandalous aftermath, and is one of our most able journalists, writers, observers and analysts. Another is C.P. Liter of the Baton Rouge States Times, who followed the whole Long era in intimate detail. (I am told he was not interviewed, though he is quoted twice in the book.) I recognize the fact that a writer cannot exhaust all sources, but there are some that should not be overlooked. In fine, his book is definitely slanted to the Long side. It has angered any number of people, on the Anti-Long side, who lived through that period, as he did not. It has been called a whitewash. One person so distraught is Harnett T. Kane who wrote <u>Louisiana Hayride</u>. *Harnett is an able reporter, knew the situation first hand, and did a splendid job with his material in his book. Williams has been careful to report on almost all of the episodes that created a sensation in the press, but to those of us who were there, it is obvious that much of what was detrimental to the Long side was swept under the rug.*

The writer seems to have a genius for describing actions and situations and positions factually, and drawing a conclusion from them completely to the contrary of what I, and I believe others, would draw, when not biased in favor of the Long side. See for example, pages 331-332.

So my conclusion on this point is that the very most favorable interpretation to the Long side of the obvious facts has been given by Professor Williams. Young people comment that they did not know Long had such stature. To those of us who were there, this seems a distortion.

The next point that disturbs me is that the book seems to be an unfair superficial and cynical treatment of the issues between the two camps, and the people on both sides. I am forced to believe there is a lack of sensitivity to the times. I, myself, do not like to be lumped

in one broad classification, with the New Or-
leans Old Regulars of that day, the stodgy
politicians, maybe honest and ineffective, the
neo-populist hillbilly of North Louisiana, (my
home area), the illiterate Cajun trappers of
South Louisiana (on whichever side they found
themselves), and the "interests", whatever
they may be. I came from an old Louisiana
family, proud of their heritage, but without any
financial means. I represented a northwest
Louisiana constituency interested in oil devel-
opment in their area, but who were agricul-
tural and small business, and my struggling
little law practice suffered from my fight
against Huey. No writer with whom I was as-
sociated in the fight, "used" by them or not, I
had the enthusiasm and idealism of youth and
was dedicated to reform. In my efforts to get a
few things done in which I was particularly
interested, I worked with others who for their
own purposes would join me. Thwarted by the
corruptionist, power hungry demagogue Long,
punished for my refusal to bow to his will, I
found myself fighting him side by side with all
others fighting him. And Williams calls us all
conservatives and Huey a liberal. I dislike
brands like this anyway, but in those days we
didn't know those terms and the issues did not
lend themselves to the present day definitions
of those terms. We spoke of radicals as against
those who believed in the American dream and
the democratic process. There were
Progressives, like John M. Parker, and good
government men in the tradition of former
Governor Luther E. Hall. We were a one party
state, but we had factions, and sometimes men

*would vote outside of the Democratic Party.
To say Long was a liberal because he said he
was for the poor man and set up the Share the
Wealth slogan suggests a contradiction. He
was like other southern demagogues and used
their tactics. He was a Hitler-like dictator, and
took away powers and rights of people to vest
them in him alone. After his regime the legislature repealed in mass those measures. This
surely is not democracy, nor does it smack of
a sincere desire to serve people. Neither is it
liberalism. Williams, himself, acknowledges
that Huey's struggle for power became an
obsession and obscured any other motivation.*

*We did not believe then that Huey had
a classifiable ideology separate from or a part
of his political ambition, which was entirely
self-centered. I cling to that belief. Williams'
page 753 is good. If a classification is necessary, I believe he was more like the populist
than the liberals of today, and I do not believe
populists were the forerunners of modern liberals. Like the populist, the core of his political strength was with the hillbilly farmers, and
he allied anyone else he could. He had some
support with labor, but that was not univer-
sal, particularly when he attacked the indus-
tries coming to the state and providing em-
ployment, so that section was divided in the
early part of his regime. Businessmen, bour-
bons, sugar planters, bankers, and organized
politicians were against him at first, but he
browbeat, bought, coerced, and maneuvered
one group after another into his camp, and
once in his camp there was no means of as-
serting any kind of independence because his*

sanctions were too severe. Thus he became dictator, and his methods were those of the demagogue and corruptionist. As I said, I like to think of myself as a reformer, but one within the framework of our democratic system. Measures I would like to have supported I could not because of his methods. With whatever good there was in a proposal, it was inextricably associated with something that added to his power, or opened the door to corruption, or was politically immoral. That is what made it impossible to go along with him, even for reform. I still believe in a lot of integrity in public life, and actually I find much of it. In spite of all I saw in that regime, and as inept and sometimes unpalatable as methods were in fighting that regime, I am still not completely cynical about politicians and public officials. Many of them are of high principle, even those with whom I disagree.

But my point here is that Williams gives the Anti-Long forces little credit for idealism, and cynically gives the impression that this was a big political fight between two equally corrupt factions, and that was all right in view of the times, and needs of people for change, and that Huey was a great champion of the people. He fails to mention the alternatives to his measures that the anti's proposed, with no success because the dictator would not let us have any credit at all, and because we included safeguards for the people's interests. I can document this statement, but in this letter, I do not want to get bogged down in detail. An example or two may be mentioned, however. One has to do with the road program. He proposed

70

enormous bond issues, and eventually used about a third of the total for corruption, and for beating the banks into submission to his political will. We proposed a pay as you go plan over which he ran roughshod. The people needed and wanted roads, but his methodology could not be followed by those of us who had our own peculiar sense of integrity. The same went for his school program. I managed to depart from my colleagues and vote for his free text books, and the only way I could do that resulted from the fact that he separated that bill from his bill providing for the funding of the program. I could stick to principle on both counts.

I believe Allan P. Sindler, in his book Huey Long's Louisiana, gives a better picture. So does Harnett Kane.

Note page 883 of Williams' book, where he refers to these two works. He ends the next to the last paragraph on that page with these words, "But in my opinion they suffer from a mechanistic view of history, from an assumption that Long was only a product and a reflection of his environment."

I do not agree that theirs is a mechanistic view of history, in his sense, because he would say, I presume, that Huey's was a humanistic effort. He may be right when he said that Long was not only a product of his environment. The word only saves his statement. Huey used the environment for his purposes, and in that sense was a product, and he had a depression for backdrop. But that was mechanistic and opportunist and not humanistic.

There is one point, however, I must mention by way of concession. That is that Huey was so smart and able and intelligent that he continually had his enemies off guard, and they underestimated him, and indeed, could not imagine that he would do the outrageous things he did, until it was too late. (I respect Russell more than his father, though Russell does not have all of his father's drives and abilities. He is a very decent person.) Huey would work day and night, all night, and all day, and possibly another night, and get drunk and sleep it off, and then he was up and at it again.

To use the word charisma in connection with Huey Long does not seem appropriate. It is true some of his followers did, in a way, worship him, but not all of them. He did have dynamism and a kind of magnetism. Everyone would acknowledge that. Sometimes his aggressive personality would be abrasive, and often interesting, and always forceful, but charismatic, no.

He had the drive of a mad man. He lacked a balance wheel and a scruple. He was completely ruthless. Williams tries to suggest now and then that he had ideals. He did express some, but none of us thought they were genuine, and his actions belied the statements. I do not pretend my side had a monopoly on all virtue nor that some of my associates were pure as the driven snow, especially in a state with a large metropolis and machine politics, and a history of possibly more than a fair share of political corruption. I do not doubt that there was too much of a double standard of hon-

esty, —one private, and the other political. But I earnestly contend that there was a group of men dedicated to the improvement of our state government, and who could not stomach Huey Long's dictatorship, method of operation, corruption, degradation of the politics of the state, his ruthlessness, and his insincerity with respect to the economic crack-pot theories of that day of depression, and these men withstood the temptations, suffered many defeats politically, economically, and in human dignity, and fought what they sincerely considered evil and dangerous and corrupt. They were supported by about one third of the population of the state, and they did the best a minority could do on the constructive side with alternatives.

As a legislator, one of my principal interests had to do with fiscal policy and the proper accounting for public money. Long wanted the free use of public money for political purposes. This led to my investigating some items and I was the first to ask the legislature to investigate. Two of the items were voted as impeachments by the House of Representatives. He defeated my bill to provide a budget system for the state, though the legislature voted for it, that is, until he got in the act and ordered the Senate to defeat it when it came up for legislative amendments. His reckless use of anyone's money, private or public, for political purposes, leads me to another observation, since I charged and proved misuse of funds. He was not avaricious in the usual sense, because he was not amassing a personal fortune as some of his followers attempted. His desires were in the direction of power, not

73

wealth, and he used, unscrupulously, money
for power, but not from avarice.

Another criticism I have of the book is
that while Williams reports what the papers
said and what the orators said on both sides,
and some of the antics of Huey, he fails to get
over what probably no writer could get over
to this generation, unless he had lived through
it, and that is the deep emotions of the day,
which were fear and apprehension. The people
of the state were like people who know the
enemy is about to invade their land and raze
their homes and loot and kill. This fear per-
vaded the state as a miasma. It was the rea-
son for some joining his forces. It was the rea-
son for many to remain silent or neutral. It
suppressed leadership. It pervaded the ranks
of his own supporters. They subjected them-
selves to his personal indignities without com-
plaint because of it. He brooked no rebuff, no
opposition, and no challenge. Huey's dicta-
torship was so absolute, people today are skep-
tical. We had said it can't happen here, but it
did.

I must recount my own experience. I
started practicing law in Shreveport in 1920. I
was having a seriously hard time. I had noth-
ing and neither did my family. In about 1921
Huey called me into his office. He was practic-
ing law and was a member of the Railroad
Commission, and very busy. He needed help,
and asked me to join him in his office. I was 22
or 23 years old, and had been there just long
enough to know his reputation at the bar. I tried
to sleep that night, and I needed an offer like
that very much. The next day I told him no. I

didn't tell him, but my reason was I would not be associated with someone whom I considered unethical. Later, in 1928 I was elected to the state legislature when he was elected governor. In the 1928 session of the legislature he asked me to vote for a certain bill. It was designed to centralize control of local bond issues in an executive office in the capitol. I told Huey I could not vote for it, because it was contrary to principles of home rule, and it centralized power in the executive. He left me in a huff. My father was getting very old, had been State Treasurer, and now was a State Bank Examiner. I went home that evening and discovered that Huey had fired him. Of course that couldn't be done because the Bank Commissioner was appointed for an overlapping six-year term. But Huey did it anyway. They dangled this job over my head the rest of my term in the legislature, very adroitly having some of their men who were my friends come to me and say, Cecil, you know you could get your father's job back. Why don't you cooperate with Huey? You are ruining your career. (The present U.S. Senator Allen Ellender, in that legislature, was one of those saying to me that I was making a mistake, ruining my future, when I could have anything I wanted.) Huey knew everyone's soft spot. This was about a year before the impeachment. I took on the financial responsibility of my family, moved them to Shreveport, and bought a little cottage where they lived the rest of their lives. We, of course, did not capitulate. But in spite of my political success in my area of Shreveport, I had trouble with my law practice because clients would frankly tell me that since

I was fighting Huey, I could not get from the state what they were entitled to, so they would have to go to someone who was in with the Longs. Of course, I continued my opposition in the special session of 1929, and our group precipitated the events that led to the impeachment, and I was active in that effort. We succeeded in persuading a reluctant house to impeach him on eight counts, and he bought his way out of the senate. Some have said that the impeachment changed him and made him vicious, as he had not been before. I think it did change him some, because for the first time he lost confidence in himself. But as to ruthlessness, total disregard for others, and a complete obsession of power, all that was there before the impeachment, so I am not sure just what is meant as to his becoming vicious only after that event. Besides, though he won the impeachment, he nonetheless was impeached by a reluctant house, and the record is replete with evidence of considerable viciousness.

And the fear and apprehension and tension grew. Harry Williams has given ultimate facts, but not that feel. And thousands noticed a relaxation and relief from tension on the faces of many of his own followers the day after Huey died. Maybe we are not sure who killed Huey. But I am sure of one thing, and that is his assassination was psychological rather than the result of specific planning. Whenever two or three were gathered together in those days, someone would say "That so and so ought to be killed." There was a lot of loose talk about the divine right of assassination. See page 717. But there was no plan that

I know of, and I do not believe there was one. But it had to happen. The tension was so great, it just took a little thing to set it off, and everyone expected it, was waiting or it, knew it had to happen. And when it did happen, everyone was worried for fear of a sort of civil war. The city of Baton Rouge was terror-stricken. For three days after the shooting, literally thousands prayed for his death.

I had gotten out of the stream of political activity at that time, having been elected to the senate in the stooge administration of O.K. Allen and was one of three votes against the administration in the senate. The other two were Boudreaux and J.Y. Sanders, Jr. Huey was controlling the state from Washington. He was still the real dictator. In the middle of that term, I was elected to the bench, the state district court in Shreveport, and I quit going to political meetings. My family and I had driven to California for our summer vacation, in 1935, and upon our return in September, just in time for court to open, we walked into the house, turned on the radio and heard that Huey had been shot. My wife was terrified, and said, "Shut the windows, pull down the shades, there will be something like a pogrom against all anti-Long people." I laughed at her, but her reaction was typical, and I felt other kinds of fears and apprehensions. There was a sort of panic, mingled with relief. The supposed assailant was riddled with bodyguard bullets on the spot, the inquest was perfunctory, witnesses testified on the radio in a sort of political field day spirit, and nothing was done about the killing of the so-called assailant. Nor could a finger be pointed at anyone else. But the book fails to give one the feel of these times.

Neither does the book place Huey in a suitable niche in history. I find little that is analytical in it, largely because he drops the story with the death of Long and does not show the results of Longism in the state or nation. I think Sindler is better. Williams fails, like the students of today, to appreciate the impact of the depression. He does do well, however, in demonstrating the challenge of Huey to F.D.R There is one deterrent that Huey suffered, and that mitigated against his fight with Roosevelt. Huey was weakening, times were changing, his sins were catching up with him, and the "Share-the-Wealth" slogan was beginning to wear out. He needed another popular issue, he was, as it were, between issues, nationally; but locally in Louisiana, he was still the King-fish and that control lasted until he died. He was a person, not an organization, so his successors failed miserably. They were lesser men and went to the penitentiary. The state came out with some roads and public works, a lot of stimulation, and an even lower political moral. There was much to be deplored in the fight between the Antis in New Orleans and the Longs. See page 715. I was glad not to be involved.

I noted many typographical errors, and one critic has written him pointing them out, to a number exceeding fifty, including the misspelling consistently of the name of the Chief Justice of the Louisiana Supreme Court. I don't know how this could have happened. I have found a few errors of fact also, and a number of omissions, but they are probably not important enough to make a point here. My own versions of some episodes would contain amplifications and variants.

The book has its virtues and is readable. But I leave it feeling unhappy with his shallow cynicism, its implications that the issues were between political factions struggling for power, in a world where all politics are dirty, and Huey was just smarter than the others, and was a great leader of the people with their interest constantly in mind.
Things were just not that way.

Sincerely yours,
Cecil Morgan

Another very similar appraisal of Huey appeared in *Biography*. "Apotheosis of Huey Long" by Glen Jeansonne.

Chapter XI

The Two Bullet Story

If one bullet was found in Huey and two bullet holes were present, then another bullet was in the abdomen. According to Merle Welsh, the mortician at the funeral home where both bodies were prepared, Dr. Clarence Lorio went to the mortuary, opened Huey, and found a bullet. This was thought to be a .45 or .38. Welsh related this story to authors David Zinman and Ed Reed. Also, author William Ivy Hair interviewed Welsh and was told the same story.

Coleman Vidrine, a cousin of Dr. Vidrine, was given a .38 slug by the doctor for safekeeping. Dr. Vidrine may have feared for his own safety. This story was related by Ed Reed on page 156 of *Requiem for A Kingfish*. The FBI report to J. Edgar Hoover stated that Huey Long was shot twice.

Some of the evidence suggests Huey was shot twice, possibly once by a .38 and once by a .45. Now, were there two men, two guns, and two bullets? It becomes very, very interesting.

I believe the doctors in the operating room knew Huey had been shot twice and that two bullets were in him or he had been shot once and had one bullet in him. Why was there a search for a bullet in the abdomen during surgery? One solid piece of material of interest to physicians was disproved as "shit.

Dr. James Starrs, a nationally known forensic scientist, who exhumed and studied Dr. Weiss' remains, conducted a taped interview with Merle Welsh. When questioned about an autopsy, Welsh said there was none. However, he did state the following: "Dr. Clarence Lorio, here in the city, M.D., a Long man and highly respected amongst Long people, came into the embalming room. He passed all the guards. I guess everybody knew him well enough. He came into the embalming room and said to me he wanted to check through Dr.

Cook's incision that he had made into Huey's side. He wanted to check that out and a few other things. Something like that - I don't know the exact words.

"I said, 'fine' and let him have it. And I just stood there and watched him. He opened up the incision because I had resutured it. He had my knives and my scalpel - anything he wanted. He spread the incision and he stuck his hand up in there, and I could tell he was exploring the cavities inside there, feeling all around and so on. He came out with a bullet. Well, he could have had that thing up his sleeve as far as I know. He came out of that incision, that body with the bullet in his hand. He said, 'There it is.' He just lay the bullet up there on that instrument tray I had on the side of the table. He lay that bullet down there and that was the last he paid any attention to the bullet."

Dr. Starrs asked, "Did he make any comment about it?"

Merle Welsh, "No, not to me."

Dr. Starrs, "Did you pick up the bullet and look at it more carefully?"

Welsh, "Well, yes, I picked up the bullet. Jack, the boy working with me, was very curious about things like that. He said, 'let me see Mr. Welsh.' Well, I let Jack check the bullet. He recognized the bullet as one that did not come out of Weiss' gun."

Dr. Starrs, "What was his last name?"

Welsh, "Umbehagen."

Welsh explained that Jack was a very good helper and continues, "but Jack wanted that. I said, 'okay you can have it.' I didn't want the bullet. I never fooled with a gun in my life. I have not even shot a gun in my life."

Dr. Starrs, "Could you tell if it was a lead bullet or was there a jacket on it?"

Welsh, "No, I couldn't tell you there, it was a high caliber bullet there, from what they tell me."

Dr. Starrs, "But he took it?"

81

Merl Welsh, "But he took it. I didn't want it. Dr. Lorio didn't care. He wanted to go on and leave that bullet there. As far as I was concerned it was his business."

Dr. Starrs, "The police weren't there right over your shoulders?"

Welsh, "No, no weren't any body stay in the room with us."

Welsh went on to say the bullet was with Umbehagen as Ed Reed investigated.

In an interview on Channel 9 TV, in Baton Rouge, Welsh implied Dr. Lorio reached high in Huey's body cavity and may have even reached into the chest cavity. In other interviews Welsh stated Dr. Lorio reached into the abdominal cavity or in the back. He was quite emphatic during these interviews and on Channel 9 TV.

Dr. Starrs asked about the bullet wound in Huey. Welsh explained that the incision of the abdomen was made through the bullet wound because he could not identify a definite bullet wound in the incision. He stated, "I couldn't see the actual hole the little bullet made because the incision obliterated the hole. But I found a hole in the back; which to my knowledge and estimation was a bullet entry and I called that to the doctor's attention, the coroner. A bullet hole along side the spine. It was a clean little, what we call in our vernacular, just a clean little entry."

Dr. Starrs, "No jagged edges?"

Welsh, "No, no jagged edges."

Dr. Starrs, "No rupture?"

Welsh, "No, no, just a clean entry."

"Now in my opinion that's where this bullet came from that Dr. Lorio fished around here and found, back in there somewhere." At this time Welsh was pointing to his waist area.

Welsh further opined, "Huey was losing blood. I say in my mind, that's where that blood was coming from. That bullet that made that hole that came in the back, it was in there and from that entry was where the hemorrhage was. That was where the blood going that Huey was supposed to be losing -from the back and that Dr. Lorio fished out of there."

Later Dr. Starrs questioned, "So the one real one that could be singled out as a bullet was in the back?"

Welsh, "Right."

The reason Dr. Lorio did not take the bullet is not understood. I could only speculate he was tired, under considerable stress, and not thinking clearly. The loss of his friend and his involvement in his care must have been depressing to him.

Chapter XII

The Automobile Enigma

Dr. Tom Ed Weiss spoke extensively to me in 1997 about the shooting. In 1935 Tom Ed Weiss was a student at LSU. He first heard of Huey's shooting when he drove by the Advocate newspaper office and noted a crowd of people. He was told of the shooting and that a Dr. Weiss was involved. He knew of two Dr. Weisses and thought first of his father. Later he went to his father's house, saw him, but their phone was dead and he could not call his brother. At brother Carl's house there were a number of unknown men about the yard and street. Entering, he told Yvonne that his brother was probably dead and she fainted.

He left with a cousin, Jim Brousseau, to find Carl's car. The family naturally was expecting a call or visit from authorities. They were never contacted. Tom Ed and Jim found the car and noted the car had been entered. The doctor's bag with instruments was in disarray. Carl's .32-caliber gun was missing from the glove compartment. A flannel sock the gun was kept in was on the floor. This led Tom to immediately think someone other than Carl had removed the gun. His brother was meticulously neat and once castigated Tom for leaving the sock on the seat and not returning it to the glove compartment when he removed the gun for his own use. The car was found after 10:30 p.m. The shooting was at 9:22 p.m.

Jim went to the Weiss home in his car to get the keys. Tom walked around the rear of the capitol and asked two policemen if they knew anything, but they would admit nothing. He saw a funeral hearse leaving the capitol, but did not stop it. This hearse probably had his brother's body. On returning to the front of the capitol, he found Carl's car had been moved. He and Jim searched for almost an hour before finding it parked some distance away. He felt he was watched and noted men in the 2nd and 3rd floors peering out the windows.

Tom Ed told me the coroner had listed Carl's personal belongings, but there were no keys in his clothes. Strange! Could someone have removed the keys, gone into the car, found the gun, and maybe even tried to place it next to the body? This is precisely what I believe happened! Tom Ed has told this story since September 8, 1935. How could Weiss provoke a shooting without a gun?

Dr. Tom Ed Weiss where he first found the car more than an hour after the shooting.

Dr. Tom Ed Weiss at the site where his brother's car was found after it was moved.

Chapter XIII

Mind Your Own Business and Keep Your Mouth Shut

Most people in the world have at one time or another been told to "mind your own business." I think this advice would help to explain the motive and reason why Dr. Carl Weiss was in the capitol building on the night of September 8, 1935. His motives and mentality were such that he had problems following this advice.

Many speculations have been made as to the motives of Dr. Weiss. One is that he pulled a short straw and was to die in order to eliminate Huey Long who was considered a tyrant. There is no evidence of this except after the shooting Long forces claimed a "Dr. Wise" was at the DeSoto Hotel, where Huey claimed plotters planned his death.

Dr. Weiss may have been upset about the Huey Long gerrymandering of the district of his father-in-law, Judge Henry Pavy. This was the most important bill on the legislative agenda that night. Uncle Henry, as I knew him, actually was nearing retirement and his salary, but not the authority or office, continued to the end of his term. Uncle Henry himself had taken this in "so called" political stride.

Another reason Dr. Weiss might have wanted to confront Huey was that he thought Huey was going to claim the Pavys had Negro blood. Twenty-five years before, a political opponent of Uncle Henry's had made this claim.

Dr. Octave Pavy, spokesman for the family, said in effect he felt Dr. Weiss could no more endure the injustice and thus had gone to the capitol that evening to confront Senator Long.

Others suggested that Dr. Weiss lived and traveled in Europe during the turmoil between the World Wars and saw first hand the tactics and development of fascism and could see Huey Long using these same tactics.

Several incidents in Dr. Weiss's life shed light on this issue. Once he was at mass and felt the priest had said something a bit unfair about someone who had arrived late for mass. He went into the rectory after the service and expressed his opinion. Another time, when in training at Bellevue Hospital in New York, he overheard a fellow physician making derogatory remarks about Jews. Although the Weiss family had been Catholic for generations, he was offended by the remarks. He rose up and turned his bowl of soup over this fellow doctor's head and even broke the bowl.

Dr. Tom Ed tells the story that, when he was in medical school, he was asked by an employee if he was the brother of Carl, who had preceded him at Tulane by over 10 years. He replied he was, indeed, Carl's brother. This person related the story that a professor once had criticized her in front of the class. Dr. Weiss, after the class, approached the professor and pointed out to him he thought the professor was unfair to the employee. An action like this was unheard of at that time.

Dr. Carl Weiss was very religious and an idealist. Once he saved a child's life by performing a penknife tracheotomy in a rural setting. The family was very appreciative and his reply was that God had helped him and given him the capabilities.

Nevertheless, Dr. Tom Ed believed that Dr. Carl had a strong pro underdog mentality. Carl felt that he could even give a powerful U.S. Senator a piece of his mind. He went to the capitol probably on the "spur of the moment." All day he had been quite content and happy with his family, not giving the slightest hint he had murder on his mind or that he would sacrifice himself.

Elemore Morgan, Sr., a well-known published photographer, was the last person to be treated by Dr. Weiss. He had tuberculosis of the throat and was on bed rest for five years. Frequently, on Sunday evenings the doctor visited at the Morgan home.

Mrs. Morgan, at an alert ninety two years of age, spoke and wrote of the doctor's visit that fateful evening of September 8, 1935. Dr. Weiss had borrowed Mr. Morgan's fishing lures and was in his usual cheerful mood. They noted no evidence of anxiety on the part of Dr. Weiss. Sometime over an hour later they learned of the shooting over the radio.

Mr. Morgan, who was not expected to live very long, survived for thirty years. Mrs. Morgan wrote of the physician, "Be assured we will always be grateful for his professional expertise and personal interest in the case which certainly got us on the right road to better things."

It's more likely that, being brushed aside by Huey Long, Weiss decided to give the Senator a fist to his lip. Not in his wildest dreams did he believe he would be killed with dozens of bullets, for not "minding his own business and keeping his mouth shut." After all, he had suffered none from confronting a priest, a professor, a fellow physician, and probably many others.

Chapter XIV

The Linney Hypothesis

Author Ed Reed in his *Requiem for A Kingfish* reports an astonishing account of the shooting as told by Douglas M. Linney to Brunswick Sholar, a Monroe attorney. It seems Linney had been in Angola Penitentiary on a gambling violation. He was from a very respectable family in North Louisiana and all his siblings had gone to college. He chose a career in oil drilling and left school early. On the night of the shooting, he was on parole and apparently, as a trustee, was assigned to the bodyguards to move about the capitol and observe people. Linney states Dr. Weiss approached Huey three times and asked to speak to him. He addressed Huey as senator twice, but the third time addressed him as governor. Huey always replied, "Later," and brushed him aside. After the third time Dr. Weiss slipped and fell to the floor. Dr. Weiss then pulled a gun and fired. It was never clear that he hit Long. Linney does not relate that Weiss hit Huey with his fist or actually shot him. His story is important because for the first time a witness claims Weiss approached Huey without a drawn gun and, not once, but three times tried to speak to him.

What is crucial here is that the solid testimony of all other witnesses is challenged; mainly, that Weiss said nothing and suddenly appeared and shot the senator in the abdomen. It just didn't happen that way.

Chapter XV

A Dynamite Affidavit

A Lafayette attorney, Tom Angers, received an affidavit from Colonel Francis Grevemberg. Grevemberg was
Superintendent of State Police during the administration of
Governor Robert Kennon. Grevemberg was anti-crime and
was known to have axed many slot machines. An article in
the Acadiana Profile summarized this affidavit. Michael
Wynne, an expert on the Longs, sent me a copy of this affidavit that Col. Grevemberg had amended and sent to him. Also,
Mike made available to me a barber's statement, which is of
interest and is also included in this chapter.

State of Louisiana
Parish of Lafayette
Affidavit of Francis C. Grevemberg

Before me, the undersigned authority person-
ally came and appeared Francis C.
Grevemberg, who, being by me first duly sworn
did depose and say that:
I served as superintendent of State
Police under the late Gov. Robert F. Kennon
during the years 1952-1955.
As a native Louisianian, I have always
had a deep interest in the late Gov. and U.S.
Sen. Huey P. Long. During my tour of duty I
had occasion to meet and work with many state
troopers who had served during Gov. Long's
statewide political career from 1928, when he
was elected governor until 1935, when he died
of gunshot wounds.
During my tour of duty the principal
priority of the State Police was the patrolling

of La. Hwys. And a massive crackdown on crime and vice in Louisiana. This included gambling, white slavery, prostitution and narcotics trafficking which was rampant in our state.

In October 1953 I decided to raid a small casino in North Louisiana. I selected four troopers to accompany me in my car. About 40 minutes into the drive, two of the three troopers seated on the back seat began reminiscing about their years on the force. Two of the men, Lt. Tugwell and Trooper Martin, said they were hoping to make 30 years before retiring.

I asked them when they first joined the force. One said the year the State Police was organized as a highway patrol. The other said he had joined a year later. I said, "You are both more than half-way. You don't have much longer to wait."

They agreed and then resumed reminiscing. They told a number of anecdotes about Gov. Long when he served from 1928 to 1932. They recalled how he used the State Police. For example, when he decided to fire a department head, he would send in a squad of troopers the night before. The department would be sealed off until the troopers had searched every file to make sure there was no piece of evidence in the files that would tend to incriminate him. After the search, Long proceeded to fire the department head.

I said nothing while they were talking. I just listened.

They continued to talk and turned to the subject of the events of September 8, 1935, when Gov. Long was shot in the State Capitol. The following is my recollection of what they said. I am combining the comments of both troopers into one narrative.

The troopers were walking behind Sen. Long and two of his bodyguards, Joe Messina and Murphy Roden, were walking on either side of him. The group was well into the hallway when a man who was standing against the side of the wall opposite the governor's office started shouting at the senator and tried to punch him in the face.

Murphy Roden grabbed the man and threw him to the floor. Almost immediately, Roden began firing at the man.

As the first bullet entered the fallen man's body, he shuddered and stretched out into a prone position against the junction of the marble floor and the marble wall. The bullets were piercing his body, striking the marble floor and ricocheting after passing through the corpse. The bullets bounced all around the hall until, all their energy spent, they would fall to the floor.

Murphy had fired about four shots when Joe Messina opened fire.

Joe Messina's last two shots hit the marble wall then ricocheted down through the man's body, struck the marble floor and ricocheted up from the floor, hitting the senator in the groin. Other bodyguards opened fire.

Both Messina and Roden emptied their .38 caliber Smith and Wesson pistols.

Soon, pandemonium broke out in the hall. Everyone was trying to escape the ricocheting bullets and there was a lot of pushing and shoving taking place as people tried to get out of the way. It is possible that all 12 bullets didn't go through the fallen man's body because the bodyguards might have been pushed while firing. This could be why Joe Messina's last two shots hit the wall and ricocheted off the floor, striking Sen. Long.

After the firing stopped, the body was searched. Papers on the body indicated that it was Carl Austin Weiss, a Baton Rouge ear, nose, and throat physician. They continued searching the body for a weapon. They found nothing.

One of the troopers in the car with me, Major John deArmond, said the night before, he was in a State Police group which had raided a barroom in Baton Rouge frequented by Negroes. When the lawmen entered, a large dice game was in progress. As soon as the raiding party shouted out that they were the state Police and it was a raid, the lights went out.

When the lights came back on, there were several switchblade knives and several revolvers and handguns on the floor. The trooper telling the story said he liked one of the handguns because it was a .25 caliber that he thought would be nice for his wife. He explained that it was in fairly good condition but it lacked a firing pin and thus it couldn't be fired. Also, there was no ammunition in the revolver.

He planned to take the handgun to a gunsmith to have it repaired and he was still carrying it on his person Sunday night, after the altercation in the state capitol. When it was determined that Dr. Weiss had no weapon on him, he offered the revolver as a "plant" or a "throw-down" to prove that the doctor actually was armed. The gun was placed in Weiss' hand by Major John deArmond.

All this happened in the corridor outside the governor's office. Sen. Long had been taken to the hospital. The trooper said that Joe Messina was very distraught and kept repeating, over and over, "I think my last two rounds hit him." The trooper telling the story said he helped pick up the spent cartridges and empty casings found.

I interrupted his narrative to ask, "Are you sure there were no other bullets or casings that somebody other than you might have found?"

Major John deArmond told me "no," adding that the items picked up from the floor constituted positive proof that the bodyguards killed both Dr. Weiss and Sen. Long.

According to the trooper, Major John deArmond, when Gen. Louis Guerre, Supt. Of State Police found out that Sen. Long had been shot with .38 caliber bullets, he returned the .25 caliber pistol that had been placed in Weiss' hand, saying that the gun was too small. He replaced the smaller pistol with a .32 caliber handgun that was taken from Dr. Weiss' car by other troopers.

One of the troopers, on the back seat, (I think it was trooper Martin) said in the early morning hours after the shooting they checked with the Motor Vehicle Bureau since they had retrieved the keys from Dr. Weiss' body and obtained the information on the license number, type of car, etc. which was registered in

Dr. Weiss' name. They went back to the Capitol grounds, found Dr. Weiss' car, and found the .32 caliber handgun in the car. He said the handgun was loaded and it was obvious that it hadn't been fired recently. He said they went back to the State Police Headquarters and gave the handgun to Gen. Guerre.

The trooper said that Gen. Guerre was emphatic that none of the bodyguards say anything about what had happened because the two bodyguards in question, Messina and Roden, could be charged with gross misconduct and even murder.

I asked the storyteller if perhaps Gen. Guerre was trying to establish Huey Long as a martyr, in the event he should die?

He told me no. He said it was simply a case of trying to protect the bodyguards who were, in turn, simply trying to protect the senator.

And then I made a mistake. I said, "It appears to me that all of the actions following the shooting were a conspiracy to cover-up the accidental death of Sen. Long and the killing of Dr. Weiss."

After I made that unfortunate statement, the bodyguards became very quiet.

The following day, I had the State Police lawyer, Drew McGinnis, on hand and I asked several of the troopers to repeat the story they had told me the previous evening. They denied that they had ever told me such a story. I called in the other troopers and they backed up what the others had said.

Later, my bodyguard and driver told me that he was sorry but he had to deny that he had heard these troopers tell that story about how Sen. Long was killed. He said it has been an unwritten law among the troopers that the Long and Weiss killings were never to be discussed. During my tenure as Supt. of State Police I had occasion to talk with other troopers who were on the force at the time of the incident. To a man, they maintained that, while they had no personal knowledge of what took place, the stories that went around the State Police were the same as I had described.

Later, I had occasion to discuss the shooting of Senator Long with a newly hired Captain of the Louisiana State Police, Capt. R.M. Walker, who was a trooper at that time, and he told me that he was present in the Troop Headquarters when the troopers were in the process of calling and talking with the Motor Vehicle Bureau and what he heard was exactly as the trooper had described it in my automobile. He said (the Captain) that it was common knowledge that one of the bodyguards had accidentally killed Sen. Long. That is, it was common knowledge among the troopers who were on the force at the time of the Weiss — Long incident.

My father was Supt. of Buildings and Grounds for the State of Louisiana under Gov. Sam Jones. Part of his responsibility was the maintenance of the State Capitol. He had been friends with Dr. Arthur Vidrine, the surgeon who operated on Sen. Long. Dr. Vidrine told my father that he removed two .38 caliber bullets from the senator's body. He was of the opinion that Sen. Long was killed by his own bodyguards, since he understood that Dr. Weiss was carrying a .32 pistol.

Actually, Dr. Weiss carried no firearm.

After the troopers refused to admit that they had told me the story or that they had heard it told to me, I called Wilburn Lunn. Wilburn was executive counsel to Gov. Kennon and was a friend of long standing. He and I had met in Italy during World War II. Colonel Lunn was full colonel executive officer and I was a lieutenant colonel G-3 in a brigade. Col. Lunn was instrumental in having Gov. Kennon appoint me to the position of Supt. of State Police.

Col. Lunn asked me to meet him in the governor's office as soon as possible. I immediately left my office to see him.

I told him the complete story of my encounter with the troopers who were with the bodyguards. He said it didn't surprise him because he had heard the same story told by different individuals. I told Col. Lunn that I needed his help to get the legislature to create a committee with full powers of subpoenas to investigate the death of Sen. Long. I told him that I wanted to question, under oath, the troopers who had told me the story, as well as anyone who was in the state capitol corridor when Sen. Long was shot.

I told him that I wanted to have Dr. Vidrine and ask him about the story that he told my father, namely that he removed two .38 caliber bullets from Sen. Long's body. I also told him I would like to have my father testify about the conversation he had with Dr. Vidrine.

I told him that, in my judgment, this was the only way he could get these people to testify truthfully — if they were under oath and subject to the state's perjury laws.

Col. Lunn told me, "Grevy, you're on the right track but your train is pulling into the wrong station."

He proceeded to tell me the uphill battle I was facing.

First, he explained, I would be facing a legislature whose membership was dominated by Long sympathizers. He continued, saying that the number of gambling raids I had conducted throughout the state had alienated local officials. Despite the prohibition against gambling in the state constitution, this vice was rampant and local officials in the state were taking bribes to allow it to continue. Col. Lunn said that legislators from these parishes would be influenced by local officials who would never be in favor of anything I proposed.

I tried to explain to Col. Lunn that I was only following the mandate of the constitution and that I always contacted local officials before conducting any raids so that they could clean up their own house by closing down illegal activities.

He interrupted me, saying, "I know all this 'Grevy', but you don't have a chance of accomplishing what you want to do. My advice to you is to forget it because I don't believe you have a prayer."

Reluctantly, I followed his advice. I dropped the matter, considering it something that was beyond my capability to do anything about.

Francis C. Grevemberg
Sept. 24, 1993

The following is an addendum sent to Wynne by Grevemberg.

June 8, 1997

At the time I gave this affidavit, when I arrived in Lafayette I didn't expect to give this statement, and I hadn't thought about it in a number of years, therefore, I wasn't certain of the names of the troopers until I had more time to reflect on the occasion. I was also able to check with my old secretary, at that time, who remembered these names, too. I am positive that Maj. John deArmond was the person on the back seat telling of the happenings, that evening, during the killing of Senator Huey P. Long by Trooper Joseph Messina. deArmond was seated immediately behind me on the right hand side of the rear seat and next to him was seated Lt. Tugwell, and to Tugwell's left was seated Trooper Martin. Sgt. Martin Fritcher was driving, and I was seated in the front passenger's seat.

Francis C. Grevemberg
June 8, 1997

I personally called Colonel Grevemberg who was quite polite to me. He stated, due to his health, he would prefer that I refer to his affidavit given to Mr. Tom Angers and, furthermore, he felt that he had nothing to add. Dr. Tom Weiss said Colonel Grevemberg was apologetic that he had not done more to help exonerate his brother. This "dynamite affidavit" of Colonel Grevemberg does many things to expose and lay bare the assassination deception. First, and most important, it supports the information given by Dr. Tom Weiss since September 8, 1935, that his brother's gun was removed from his car which obviously had been tampered with, left in disarray, and even moved. Next, I feel it destroys the very easily contrived unanimous argument that Weiss said not a word and suddenly shot Senator Long. In this affidavit we learn that Weiss did apparently try to, or actually did, hit Senator Long and probably offered to fight with the bodyguards. The firing occurred with many people in close quarters. Further, it explains how the bodyguards and General Louis Guerre, Head of what was the Criminal Bureau of Investigation in 1935, obtained information as to Weiss' identity and his auto license plate number from the License Bureau. The Criminal Bureau of Investigation was the predessessor to the Louisiana State Police. Grevemberg states this happened in the wee hours of the morning. Dr. Tom Ed, however, claims he found the car about one hour and fifteen minutes after the shooting. There was plenty of time after the shooting for these events to have happened.

The following letter from barber Morris Soileau was sent to Colonel Grevemberg.

Assassination of Huey P. Long

I was lucky enough to have my barbershop near the Louisiana State Police Headquarters, and I got to be well acquainted with the high ranking officers, some of whom were Huey Long's bodyguards. Two of them started talking; they were the only customers at the time. I've always wanted to know the real story, so I was getting it first hand. One was showing the end of his finger where it was shot off during the shooting (they are both dead now). They had ask not to reveal their names or the story, but it's something that history is wrong

102

about. I will tell you why after I tell you the actual story.

It was said that the judge Pavey family had negro blood in them which was not true. They were just dark complexed people. Dr. Wiess a Baton Rouge Dentist, had married judge Pavey's daughter, so he took offense to Huey saying the Paveys had negro blood, so he went to the capital and waited in the coridor at the governs elevator as Huey steped out of the elevator Dr. Wiess took a swing at Huey and the body guards threw him on the floor. Joe Mesina had a .38 cal. Machine gun and riddled the Dr.'s body, bullets were flying everywhere on the marble walls and floor. Two of the bullets came from the floor and hit Huey in the lower abdominal severing an artery, he began bleeding very much and was taken to the Our Lady of the Lake Hospital, but he would'nt let any doctor touch him. He wanted Dr. Vidrine who was in New Orleans, head of Charity, who Huey had appointed. So Huey died from loss of blood. In the meantime Joe Mesina who had taken a small 32 cal. Handgun off a negro in a crap game the night before, by the way the gun had no firing pin. He put the gun in Dr Wiess's hand so history would say Huey was killed by an assassin and not by the hands of his own men, this would make him more of a hero. History will never know because all who witnessed the true story are now dead. I believe it is the most logical story ever heard or read about.

I have heard many other stories about Louisiana politicians and governors. I wanted to write a book on it because most people don't want to know the real truth.

Grevemberg stated the barber blacked out the last sentence because it named Roden and Messina.

Chapter XVI

A Trail to Texas

Dr. Tom Ed Weiss allowed me to read a letter from a Mr. Aris A. Mallas, sent to the TV program "Unsolved Mysteries." "Unsolved Mysteries" reviewed the shooting but the program added nothing to the debate. A reporter, a good friend of Mallas, was a witness to the Huey Long shooting. Mr. Vernon McGee, the reporter, has a son, Dr. Gordon McGee, who is a pathologist in El Paso, Texas. I spoke to him and he confirmed that Mr. Mallas had quite an illustrious responsible background and was indeed close to his father, who at one time was employed by Mr. Mallas. Dr. McGee thinks his father may have felt a bit of shame for never reporting the affair because he was a man who was always proud of his integrity. He also thought his father was actually sent from Texas to report on the Long political doings in Louisiana because other reporters were either intimidated or bought off. I phoned Mr. Mallas and he sent me a similar letter which strongly supports Colonel Grevemberg's affidavit. This is evidence on top of evidence. This interesting letter is as follows:

7 May 1997

Dr. Donald A. Pavy
111 Stevens Street
New Iberia, LA 70560

Dear Dr. Pavy:

I am sorry it took so long for me to answer your letter of March 18, 1997, but I have such a flood of correspondence it is hard for me to be timely.

RE MYSELF: Brief data sheet is attached.

RE MR. VERNON McGEE:

I first met him when I came to Texas in 1953 to direct the largest hospital study ever undertaken in the world (25,000 beds). McGee was Director of the Legislative Budget Board, our all-powerful fiscal agency for state government. He held that position for 17 years, which is by far the longest tenure of anyone.

McGee came up through the news wire services. He was a Vice President of the Kiplinger News Service and his first wife was the one that gave the name to Kiplinger's "Changing Times". Since we had many mutual interests due to the research I was doing, we got to know each other quite well. In following through on that research effort we would sometimes travel together by car in West Texas where you can go for hours and not see much.

On one such boring trip he told me he wanted to tell me something he had told no one since he was fearful of his life and that of his family, BUT I could never tell anyone. When I agreed to these conditions he told me the following. (Until I saw the presentation of the Long shooting on Unsolved Mysteries I never mentioned this account to anyone, but I suddenly realized that McGee was dead, his first wife was dead and children were long ago grown up and far distant. Therefore, I felt these facts should be known to others.)

THE EVENT:

Mr. McGee was a reporter in the news set-up (I think INS) at the state capitol in Ba-

ton Rouge, the day of the shooting. There was a lot going on and the various reporters for the wire services, including McGee, were following Long around. As the group...this included Long, some staff, and a group of state police bodyguards...went down the hall with the governor in the lead...everyone stopped since a man came up to speak with Long. McGee says Long brushed off the man and rudely pushed him away. As he did so the bodyguard immediately in front of McGee pulled his side arm and it hung in the holster. When he jerked it free it cocked, fired and, to McGee, it appeared to hit Long in the back...sort of the kidney area.

McGee says it was obvious the young man did not plan to fire, but only to have his side arm ready. When he did fire, that shot caused the other bodyguards to shoot at the person pushed back by Long. He was killed and the reporters were kept back away from the body. McGee thought the man was unarmed since he never saw a gun nor did he see or hear any threat. It seemed to him the fellow was just trying to talk with Long.

When the reporters were told to stay away and to return to their news office immediately, they did so. In a matter of minutes the head of the state police appeared and made it very clear that there had been an assassination attempt on Long and the bodyguards had killed the assassin AND they wanted no change in that story or there would be serious consequences. (McGee never did detail what they were, but only indicated life was at stake.)

McGee told me this story three times over a period of 15-20 years. The first time at his choice of time and place and the other two times I would edge into the topic. He was always under great stress and clearly felt it was dangerous to tell what really happened. The last time we discussed it was when he was serving as top administrative assistant to Governor (Texas) Smith. When he left the Legislative Budget Board he came to work for my research company and when Gov. Smith needed his long experience we gave him a leave of absence to assist the Governor.

At that final session I asked him why he was still fearful since so much time had gone by. He said, "I haven't given you all the details, but it was very clear that one told the true facts at risk of their life at any time."
OTHER DETAILS:

Vernon outlived his first wife so she might have known the story, but is no longer available. His second wife, who lives in Austin, I knew her back in the 60's, but have not seen her since. Dr. Weiss talked with her and I believe McGee's son who is a M.D. in El Paso, Texas. He might have some knowledge from those conversations. One other knew the story since he was my #2 man for 42 years, but he is now hospitalized and has lost most of his memory.

OTHER: I do not have a high regard for your state police. Back in the 1970's I designed and directed a several day in-service training session for the Criminal Justice officials of the states of: Texas, New Mexico, Okla., La & Arkansas. A great many of the

*State Police attended in each state and I would
have rated the quality of professionalism of
the LA group at the bottom of the five states. I
hope in the past 20 years they have improved.*
*IN ANSWER TO YOUR OTHER
QUESTIONS:*
*He did relate that Dr. Weiss tried to
speak with Long, but no mention was made of
his trying to hit him on the lip. Remember,
McGee was behind the group. I wrote to Unsolved Mysteries and they forwarded the letter to Dr. Weiss.*
*Feel free to use the above in any way
that you wish. My only interest is that the Weiss
family has suffered from what is, if you follow
the facts as given me by McGee, an injustice
that needs to be corrected. I am only interested in trying to be helpful.*
*If you have any further questions I will
be glad to assist.*

*Sincerely,
Aris A Mallas
Chairman of the Board*

Dr. Tom Ed Weiss phoned the widow of Vernon
McGee. She stated that Vernon told her Weiss did not shoot
Huey Long, but she gave no details.

It is strange that of all the reporters in the Capitol none
even acknowledged they were ever near the shooting. If any
had seen the shooting, they no doubt always pictured the horror of that evening in their minds. Certainly no one wanted to
be the recipient of the generous amount of lead that was so
capably donated to Dr. Weiss.

The discrepancy that Huey was shot by two errant
bullets or shot in the back by bodyguard, Messina or Roden,

exists. My only explanation would be that in a closed area few could see all that happened in a matter of seconds. Messina would have been reluctant to take the blame for a more stupid accidental direct shot into Huey's back. He would more likely have admitted to a ricochet bullet! Also, how could he have seen or known which ricocheted bullet hit Huey.

Some believe the Mafia or President Franklin Roosevelt had Huey sent to his Maker. One bodyguard could have intentionally shot Huey in the back and then claimed to his coworkers, who were unable to see all that happened, that errant bullets got Huey. Further, Weiss would have been the pigeon. I do not believe this scenario.

Reporter Vernon McGee who related to Mallas that he had witnessed the shooting.
Courtesy of Dr. Gordon McGee.

Chapter XVII

Nice Guys:

Dr. Carl Adam Weiss had one encounter with then Governor Huey Long. It seems Huey had a foreign body in his eye and came to the elder Dr. Weiss's office. He was a difficult patient and used considerable profanity. Huey was amused when his bodyguards or friends dropped cotton balls on the floor so as to observe the very attractive and shapely nurse bend over to pick them up. After the treatment Dr. Weiss addressed the governor in no uncertain terms. He warned Huey that he was never again welcome in his office unless he conducted himself as a gentleman.

It wasn't until December 8, 1985 that The New Orleans Times Picayune reported information the Weiss family had know since 1935. Dr. Dudley Stewart, an orthopedic surgeon in New Orleans and a close friend of Dr. Weiss, phoned the Weiss family within hours of the shooting. The family thought their phone had been tapped. The very next day Dr. Stewart was beaten in his office by two state policemen in an attempt to force him to sign a statement that Weiss was a socialist. He refused to sign and called a doctor he knew to be strongly pro-Long. The policemen departed after talking to the physician on the phone.

The next day two different policemen came to his office with a warrant charging him as an accessory to the shooting. They tried to force him to sign a statement that he and Weiss discussed the shooting in a car on Marengo St. The policemen claimed Weiss stated he had pulled a short straw and thus was chosen to kill Huey Long. Dr. Stewart was again abused. It stopped only after he called the same physician as before and asked him to intercede. Dr. Stewart feared for his life and only revealed this story fifty years later.

The Weiss family feared for their own safety. They spent a week in seclusion in a New Orleans hotel after the funeral on Monday, September 9.

Uncle Henry did not attend the funeral of his son-in-law on Monday, September 9, 1935, because he was too depressed. He stayed in his home with my father who sedated and consoled him. While sitting on the front porch a discussion ensued between Uncle Henry and my father about what Huey would do to the Pavy family if he were to live. They wondered what sort of vindictive retribution he would devise.

Chapter XVIII

Two Jax Beers

Joe Messina was Huey's top bodyguard and a very interesting character who played an important role in the shooting. He was dark, short, very strong, and handy with his fists. He carried a black jack and a pearl-handled pistol. He worshipped Huey, served as a sort of valet, attending to his Master's every wish, and was always next to him. Joe was rather slow mentally and was thought to have suffered "shell shock" in World War I. Huey sometimes made fun of Messina. Once, when LSU football players were concerned about the size and talent of an upcoming opponent, Huey assured them that Joe Messina had checked on these players and LSU had nothing to fear.

After Huey's death it was rumored that Messina had been placed in an institution because he was constantly crying and lamenting that he had shot his best friend. I contacted a member of Messina's family and she stated to me that he was not in an institution but owned some type of business in the Gonzales area. I have reason to believe her. During the inquiry by District Attorney Odom, Messina was quite depressed and stated that he had lost his best friend.

Delmas Sharp, Sr. was a bodyguard of Huey Long. Through his granddaughter I located Delmas Sharp, Jr., who lives in Tulsa, Oklahoma. It seems that Delmas Sr. knew Messina very well. There was an Ed Sharp who was a bodyguard in the capitol on September 8, but he did not see the shooting. He testified at the D.A.'s inquiry. According to Delmas Jr., his father was not in the building at the time of the shooting.

Delmas Sharp, Jr. wrote me a letter telling what he knew about the shooting. I feel it is very important because it is a happening that he himself experienced. I was greatly impressed with this gentleman, an ex marine, who was "all business." He was very emphatic that he did not expect me to misquote him in any way.

The following is Delmas Sharp Jr.'s statement.

6305 S 70 E. Ave.
Tulsa, OK 74133-4058
October 4, 1998

Dr. Donald Pavy
111 Steven St.
New Iberia, LA 70560

Confirming our telephone conversation at 9:15, Sunday, 10/4/98...

 In the early spring of 1951, on Saturday morning, my father said I should go with him down the airline Highway from Baton Rouge, La. toward New Orleans. He said since I was graduating from LSU and would be going away in the military, he wanted me to know about Huey Long's killer. On the way, he said Joe Messina was one of Huey's bodyguards and was the one who shot Huey, and he wanted me to see and meet Joe.

 In a swampy stretch of the highway, on the east side, across a canal, there was a roadhouse (honky-tonk). We crossed a wooden bridge across the canal to the roadhouse. Dad pounded on the door. A voice from inside said, "I'm closed." My dad said, "Joe, open this door." When the man inside opened the door, my dad said, "Hello, Joe. My son and I would like a beer." Dad and I walked to the bar and took a seat and Dad ordered 2 JAX beers. Dad said I was going away and he wanted me to meet Huey's killer. The man turned his back

toward us and said nothing. In a few minutes,
the man, with his back toward us said, "you
got your beer, so just go." Dad said we might
like a refill on the beers, but the man kept his
back toward us and said nothing.

So Dad and I left. Dad said to me,
"well, that's Joe Messina, the killer."

Delmas O. Sharp, Jr.

I found two sisters in Gonzales, Louisiana, who, when young, worked for Messina. They stated he had a filling station with a small restaurant, a bar, and dance hall. It was located on Airline Highway between Gonzales and Sorrento.

They liked the Messinas and spoke well of them. Mrs. Messina was a pretty lady and very religious. They knew Messina was an ex-bodyguard of Huey but they knew nothing of the shooting.

Delmas Sharp, Sr., bodyguard who identified Messina as the
one who shot Huey Long.
Courtesy of Mary Beth Orr

Joe Messina, bodyguard of Huey Long and always near him.
Courtesy Russell Billiu Long Papers, Mss. 3700, Louisiana
and Lower Mississippi Valley Collections, LSU Libraries,
Louisiana State University, Baton Rouge, Louisiana

Chapter XIX

The Roden Story

According to testimony of witnesses, Murphy Roden was the most heroic of the bodyguards. He wrestled with Weiss and one account has it Weiss may have shot Roden's watch. Also, he was the first to shoot Weiss. Roden was probably the brightest of the bodyguards and served in responsible positions later in life. He was a close friend of Senator Russell Long. The story was told that he saw Huey off on a train in Washington and rode his motorcycle all the way to Louisiana, arriving before the train.

Now, years later, with much effort and searching, I have located and spoken to members of the Roden family. They were very courteous and successful people but revealed nothing. One stated that he only knew that Murphy fired first, but nothing indicating if it was before, after, or rather than, Weiss.

Finally, I found and met Loretta "Lo" Spurlock, formerly married to a relative, Jerry Roden. I also spoke several times to Jerry Roden, Jr., who now lives in Georgia. They spoke freely and candidly about what they think they know about the shooting.

The following are the letters of Loretta Spurlock and Jerry Roden, Jr.:

I, Loretta Spurlock, state the following facts freely and they are what I know to be the truth.

I was married to Jerry Roden, Sr., for 20 years, having two children from this union. We were divorced in 1974. He was the nephew of Murphy Roden well known as a bodyguard of Senator Huey P. Long. I never did actually meet Murphy Roden. The Roden family I knew were not close to each other.

Some few years into our marriage when Jerry, Sr. was working as a policeman, he had a discussion about Murphy with other lawmen. At that time he told me that Murphy had accidentally shot Huey Long.

He also stated this to our two children and we were all told that this is a subject we must never discuss. The older child, Jerry, Jr., was curious and asked his grandmother, Mrs. Lizzie Bert Roden about this fact. She always avoided a discussion and said that no one was to discuss this, but she did not actually deny the fact. My mother-in-law was, of course, married to Wilbur Roden, a brother of Murphy Roden.

I write this because history has been distorted by the confusion in the facts about the Huey Long shooting. I hope this will help to bring forth the truth.

Loretta Spurlock

Dr. Donald Pavy
111 Steven Street
New Iberia, LA 70560

I declare that between the ages of 10 and 13 that my father related to me the following:
That Murphy Roden is a blood relative of ours;
That he was (at that time/is) an uncle to my father and a great uncle to me;
That he was a bodyguard of former governor Huey P. Long;
That he shot Huey Long by accident one night during a fracas at the capitol;

*That it was an accident and very few people
know of this;*
*When I attempted to speak to my grandmother
about this, she told me to change the subject
as we do not speak of that in the family;*
I make these statements freely and voluntarily.
I hold responsible all parties who would misuse this information or this statement.
*My understanding is that this information is
for literary purposes only.*

Sincerely,
Jerry Roden
1091 Fountain Lake Dr
Brunswick, GA 315425
Witness: Carol Criss

I did an extensive genealogy research of the Roden family. Wilbur Roden was not a brother and very likely not even a first cousin. He may have been a more distant cousin. I print these letters because this family may have in some way received information about Murphy. It does appear that we were on the right track about Huey being shot accidentally!

Chapter XX

In Vino Veritas

Often people, when relaxing and drinking, may reveal deceptions or speak with accuracy. It was under these circumstances that one of the more amazing revelations of the shooting came about. "In vino veritas" was first used by Plato. It means, in wine is the truth.

Gerard Fournet, a druggist in Franklin, Louisiana, heard of my book one evening at a dinner we were both invited to by mutual friends, Gene and Anne Patout. He then revealed to me his conversation years ago with Justice John B. Fournet. This information I determine as very important because Judge Fournet was, as a witness, the highest ranking official of the Long administration, and later, as Chief Justice of the State Supreme Court, his testimony was unlikely to be questioned. His career was quite interesting; he had served in the Legislature as Speaker of the House and also in the Executive Branch, as well as Chief Justice of the State Supreme Court. The following is the sworn statement of Gerard Fournet.

August 14, 1997

This is a story that was told to me, to the best of my recollection, by John B. Fournet, former Chief Justice of the Louisiana Supreme Court, on June 11, 1955, at what is now known as the "Fournet House" in St. Martinville, LA. The house is located at 109 East Clairbone, on the south side of the St. Martin Parish courthouse and was the residence of the family of Mrs. John B. (nee Sylvia Fournet) Fournet. The home of Mrs. Fournet's family was the setting for a celebration honoring William Briant

Webb on the occasion of his Baptism.

His parents were Sydney Briant (Jackie) Webb and Joan Irene Sesher Webb. 'Jackie' was raised in the home by the grandfather of Sylvia, Margaret and Rowena Fournet who were all present, along with other family members including the Chief Justice.

I had met the Chief Justice on two previous occasions, and I was telling him that I recently had the opportunity to meet a friend of his on the military base where I was stationed on Long Island, NY. When I told him that the person whom I had met was Colonel Roden, who was a brother of former Louisiana Governor Huey Long's friend and bodyguard, Murphy Roden with the Louisiana State Police, Justice Fournet's face lit up like a boy remembering his college days. Justice Fournet, who is a distant relative of his wife Sylvia (as well as a distant relative of mine) and me, was really the contemporary of my uncle, Msgr. Lawrence Martin Fournet.

Colonel Roden was the only person we (JBF and I) had in common and I was very happy, as a young Army officer, to be able to relate my meeting with his friend. Although Colonel Roden must have believed that I was a close relative of Justice Fournet, it was surely comforting to have his Sergeant-Driver deliver <u>The Times Picayune</u> to my BOQ on Long Island every Sunday morning.

Chief Justice Fournet was happy to hear that his name was so honored by his friend's brother. At this point, he invited me to sit with him in the next room, where it was somewhat cooler and away from the crowd.

122

The ceiling fan and the French Champagne created a most relaxed atmosphere; and this is where he began to relate to me this amazing and unexpected story.

Judge Fournet began by telling me about his relationship to Captain Murphy Roden and Huey P. Long. He became melancholy and began to relate the events that transpired in the Capital of Louisiana in Baton Rouge on that unforgettable day in September, 1935. He talked of their conversations in the governor's office.

He said, "Senator Long, Captain Roden and I were leaving the Governor's office. Captain Roden left first, Senator Long followed him out of the door and I was walking behind the Senator. As the Senator went through the door, I heard a shot and then I saw him falling to the floor. Murphy Roden grabbed him under the arms, and I held his feet..."

At this point, Judge Fournet realized that other people had come into the room and were listening to him and so, he stopped talking. I had been so fascinated by his 'histoire' that I failed to notice the gathering which had assembled.

Judge Fournet did not indicate to me that he saw anyone shooting.

Thus done and signed at Franklin, St.Mary Parish, Louisiana, on this 7th day of August, 1997, in the presence of Leigh L. Charpentier and Wendy Boudreaux, two witnesses who have signed these presents with said preparer and me, Notary, after due reading of the whole.

There is one point of interest here. Justice Fournet may not actually have witnessed the shooting. This breaks the solidarity of the witnesses stating that Weiss appeared suddenly and did not say a word, produced a gun and shot Huey Long.

I believe during the eight days between the shooting and the District Attorney's hearing the deception was carefully planned by the Long faction and each person's statement was determined. Their "veritas," however was undone by the "vino."

The point here is: Did Weiss cause a scene and hit Huey, which activated the events described by Grevemberg and Mallas? Apparently he did and Fournet and other witnesses made efforts to absolutely discredit the behavior or action of Weiss leading to the shooting. It is ludicrous to think Weiss shot Huey and also hit him.

In the video, "The Kingfish and Uncle Earl," Mr. Tom Votier, son of bodyguard Paul Votier, quotes his father as saying that Justice Fournet did not hit the gun of Dr. Weiss. He does claim his father stated he was next to Huey and saw the actual flash of the gun when Weiss shot Huey.

Chapter XXI

An Elevator Ride

When I interviewed scrub nurse Melinda Delage, who was present at Huey Long's operation, she told me about Zilma Aubin Utz, a young nursing student who was the first to receive Huey in the hospital. Ms. Utz sent me a letter about her experience. She stated that history has recorded another nurse on the floor was first to see Huey in the hospital. She disputes this and writes the following:

March 25, 1998

Dear Dr. Pavy:

The following statement is my involvement and recollection of events in the Long shooting.

On September 8, 1935, as a student nurse at Our Lady of Lake Hospital, I went on duty as charge nurse on first and second floors at 9:00 p.m. There were no patients on first floor that night. Second floor was used for medical diseases. The emergency and ambulance entrance was in the back of the hospital at the end of the first floor hall and was kept locked. There was a loud doorbell outside of the locked door. The night supervisor, who was a nun, was supposed to answer the bell if someone needed admittance through the emergency entrance. If she could not get there soon enough, the student nurse from the first and second floor would answer. The patient would then be taken to the emergency room, which was on the first floor.

125

The emergency room was an ordinary room about the size of other patient rooms. The nurse did whatever was necessary for the patient and then would go to find the nun. There were no phones open on this floor at night. Baton Rouge was a small town back then and there was no need for a fully manned emergency room. There was no desk at the door and admissions were processed in the office on second floor. The nun could take charge, call the doctor, and admit the patient. Doctors would come in about ten minutes after being called.

At about 9:35 a.m. or so the emergency room doorbell rang. I was out in a patient's room doing temperature reduction measures on a child. As soon as I could I ran down the stairs. I could hear loud voices and noises inside the door. There were two or three men who had taken the door off at the hinges and were putting a man on a stretcher. They were just putting his left leg on the stretcher when I arrived. I saw it was Senator Huey Long.

The men were nervous and very excited. I took them to the emergency room. I didn't see anything that I could do except call the nun. They said, "We'll use your house doctor." They didn't know any local doctors. I left them to go find the nun upstairs and she was nowhere to be found. I heard more noises, ran down, and saw them at the elevator with the patient. They wanted to go to the operating room, but didn't know where to go. They got me to go with them. The elevator was not used at night except for patients.

The noise brought the nun to us at the elevator as we got to the fourth floor. She sent me back to my station. She then took Huey back to third floor, undressed him, admitted him, and called doctors, surgical (student) nurses, and externs who worked at the hospital that summer.

While I was in the elevator with Huey, I stood at Huey's right side next to his abdomen. I said, "What is wrong with him?" They said he had been shot. I asked who shot him and they said Dr. Carl Weiss. Huey's eyes were open but he never said a word the whole time. He was pale; I think his lips were a little pink. I saw no blood anywhere, no torn clothes, no holes like a shot, or any other evidence of injury.

One of the men who was consoling Huey leaned down and kissed him on the cheek. By this time we were on the fourth floor where the operating room was located. The nun arrived just as we got off of the elevator, which is when she took over and sent me back to my station.

The hospital was put under strict security from then on. Guards blocked the entrances and exits. The Long family and the doctors had a private entrance on the first floor. Streets were closed. The next night when I went back on duty, the halls were crowded with reporters and probably other dignitaries. Student nurses were not allowed to talk with these people. We got news from the newspaper and from other students. When Huey was laid out in the Rotunda of the Capitol the students were allowed to go in uniform to view the body.

Zilma Aubin Utz

127

One thing of significance is that Huey knew his assailant when he reached the hospital, which suggests Weiss may have introduced himself. This seems to contradict the statements that Weiss uttered not a word and was unknown to Huey.

Of profound significance is the statement that Utz was less than a foot from Huey's right upper abdomen, even hovering over him, and she observed nothing. This suggests no abdominal gunshot wound was present. She did fail to recognize a lip injury, only noticing that the lips were "a little pink." There were, however, other accounts of the lip wound.

Nurses Melinda Delage and Zelma Utz

Chapter XXII

Scientific Snooping

In 1991 Professor James E. Starrs, with Weiss family approval, assembled an impressive group of scientists to exhume and study in exquisite detail the remains of Dr. Carl Weiss. This was all done at no cost to the Weiss family. There was a toxicologist, a medical examiner, a ballistics expert, and an anthropologist from the Smithsonian Institute. Starrs himself is a renowned professor of forensic science at George Washington University in Washington, DC. He is also a lawyer and a DNA expert. He is well known for his studies on the remains of Zachary Taylor, Jesse James, and others. He is an avid cyclist who cycles daily to his office and has traveled across the entire country on his bike. Dr. Tom Ed Weiss asked him where he spent the nights when cycling. His reply was, "usually in a cemetery because no one bothers me there."

This investigation found the long lost .32-caliber pistol belonging to Weiss. A search of the will of General Louis Guerre, Superintendent of the State Police, revealed the whereabouts of the gun. The gun and bullets, (six in a clip, and one fired) were in the possession of Mrs. Mable Guerre Binnings, the general's daughter. Also, of very great importance was finding police records, crime scene photographs, and pictures of Huey's garments with bullet holes. Dr. Carl Weiss, Jr. sued for ownership of the gun and was awarded custody. The gun is now in the Old State Capitol Museum.

The fired bullet caused excitement. People thought it was indeed the bullet that traversed Huey's body. Ballistic studies proved that the spent slug was not fired from the Weiss gun.

In Carl Weiss, Jr.'s letter to me about his father, he wrote the following:

He and my mother had "plinked" at targets

*in the Amite River where they had a camp,
which they had visited on the day he died. This
same gun came into the possession of Col.
Guerre, the Chief of the State Police, and he
left it to his daughter, Mabel Binnings. The
existence of this weapon was mentioned to me
by Russell Long, who had no interest in it, as
we breakfasted once in NYC. The matter was
later pursued by James Starrs, the forensic
attorney, who sent an investigator to her and
offered her a considerable sum of money
($15,000), which she declined. She left no
doubt, however, that she had the weapon in
her possession and it later appeared in her
bank vault in New Orleans.*

*Ownership of this gun involved a
lengthy legal battle in which I prevailed, as
she had no claim to the weapon, which her
father had retained as a part of his ex-officio
"investigation" of the deaths. I eventually
donated the gun to a museum-like collection
in Baton Rouge. Tom Ed has seen it displayed
there with what I believe to be a non-specific
caption identifying it as my father's gun. This
of course could be a chapter in itself as it took
quite a bit of time and money and was rela-
tively fruitless. I fired the gun a few times in
Opelousas and saved a few copper-jacketed
71 grain slugs, and was glad to be rid of it.
Ironically, Judge Pavy had confiscated a similar weapon (.32-cal. Savage which had been
a murder weapon) which I still possess.*

The remains removed from a Baton Rouge cemetery
were brought to the Lafayette medical examiner's facility. I
joined the scientists in their initial appraisal of the remains

and in the review of the x-rays. We had lunch and I observed the news conference the next day. I was very impressed.

The bones and clothes were intact. Peculiarly, the hair was all-intact, still attached to thin leathery skin. The Weiss remains and x-rays were all sent to the Smithsonian Institute. There they reconstructed every bone and determined the direction of each shot. These shots came from all directions but mostly Weiss was shot in the back. Most interesting were the studies done on a .38-caliber bullet found in the skull. This bullet had entered through the eye. It had fibers on it consistent with the doctor's shirt. There were also bullets that hit an arm and wrist. The conclusion was that Weiss was attempting to protect himself and thus in a defensive stance when shot, protecting his head with his hand.

Chapter XXIII

"Distressing"

I studied the crime scene photographs now located in the Louisiana State Archives. Pictures of the dead Weiss are very significant because no gun was seen in any of the photographs presented to me. Two separate photographs of the gun were in the collection, but it is obvious the photos of the gun were not taken on the marble floor at the site of the shooting. No blood is found on or about the gun. The obvious reason the gun was not included is that the crime photos were taken before the gun was taken from the glove compartment of the car. Recall that Tom Ed saw the ambulance leaving when he first found the car and walked around the side of the capitol. This was probably less than two hours after the shooting. Had Carl Weiss shot Huey as many witnessed, why was his gun not on the scene? Also, why weren't pictures of the gun on the scene taken on the marble floor instead of on a neutral white background?

I phoned David Zinman and inquired about his efforts to find crime scene photos. He said he could not find any when he first studied the case. About the same time, Herman Deutch produced a picture of the Weiss body. Zinman only recalls he saw this in his book, *The Huey Long Murder Case*. Ed Reed did not mention crime scene photographs in his book. Reed confirmed that the crime scene photographs were placed in the Louisiana State Archives after being found in the possession of Mable Guerre Binnings in the early 1990's.

The pictures of Huey's garments and statements of witnesses were the basis for "The Final Investigative Report: Senator Huey Long", which was published by the Louisiana State Police in June 1992. They made a statement that, "The lack of any chain of custody on any of the evidence is distressing." Tampering with clothing could be possible. Not finding the gun in the crime scene should also have been "distressing" to the state police. This was not mentioned in their report. In the photos of Weiss, which I reluctantly reproduced, spattered blood can be seen on the pillars. This fact would support the conclusion that Weiss was shot exactly where his body was photographed. The gun should have been near. Why was crime scene evidence not presented in 1935?

The following quote is taken from Professor James Starr's letter sent to me: "The failure to find a gun in any of the photographs of Dr. Weiss signifies either that he had drawn no gun or that his gun was removed from or about his person before the photographs were taken. Since photographs were taken of Dr. Weiss in the corridor, in various poses, it seems obvious that the police were memorializing the situation according to the regular investigative protocol. Consequently, you are right, in my estimation, in reading the lack of any gun on or about Dr. Weiss as strong circumstantial proof that he had not drawn a gun in the affray in the corridor. I thank you for giving me the opportunity to comment on this new and significant observation, on which you seem to be the first to give attention."

The Louisiana State Police should go back to the drawing board and produce another "Final Investigative Report." Sincere efforts, no doubt, would lead to much more "distressing" findings!

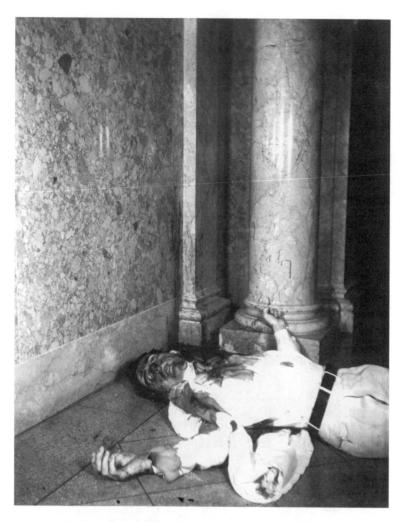

Crime photograph of the body of Dr. Carl Austin Weiss where it lay shortly after the shooting. This photograph and others like it were found as a result of efforts by Carl Weiss, Jr. to find the .32 caliber gun. Only author Herman Deutch had access to them until they were found in 1991 in the possession of Mable Guerre Binning.

Courtesy of Louisiana Department of State, Division of Archives, Records Management and History

These two photographs from the Louisiana Archives were obviously not taken at the crime scene because they were not photographed on a marble loor. This evidence supports the conclusion that this gun was not at the crime scene at the time of the shooting.

Courtsey of Louisiana Department of State, Division of Archives, Records Management and History

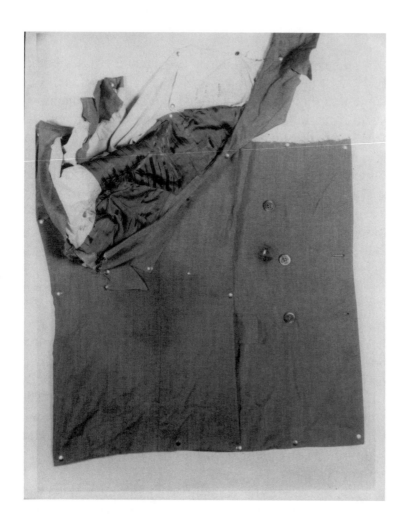

Alleged coat of Senator Huey Long with bullet hole and powder burn.
Courtesy of Louisiana Department of State, Division of Archives, Records Management and History

Chapter XXIV

Political Version

I have previously alluded to the inquiry of September 16, 1935. It has been the basis of declarations by the Long people that there was an "Official" version. No conclusion was drawn from this. No judicial ruling or statement was made. There was no physical evidence or cross-examination. No indictment of Weiss was made. This, then, was entirely political and not official. To prove the so-called "official version" is pure politics, I have requested the legal analysis of an experienced and respected lawyer, Alfred "Smitty" Landry. No such detailed attempt to legally dissect the "official version" has ever been done.

The following chapter is his professional appraisal:

On September 10, 1985, fifty years to the day after the death of his father, Huey P. Long, Russell Long introduced into the Congressional Record a document which purports to be a transcript of a Coroner's Inquest over the body of Dr. Carl A. Weiss, including questions to witnesses. The recorded comments of Russell Long that accompany the transcript (a record that was "lost" for many years) are intended by the son as an apologia on the life, political career, and death of the father.

The son gives his unqualified endorsement to the witnesses, whose testimony was recorded, commenting on their successful careers in politics and other fields. He states, "Mr. President, I knew these people and in my judgment these people told the truth." The problem here is that he pits the moral fiber, credibility, and integrity of these "people" (all political) against the word of others (many apolitical) who offer considerable information that exonerates Dr. Weiss. This information, voluntarily offered by impartial observers of the shooting, the hospitalization, and the surgery performed on Huey Long, lend credence to the conclusion that Huey was accidentally shot and that Dr. Weiss himself was slaughtered without a gun in his possession.

Several pages of Senator Long's statement into the Congressional Record are devoted to Huey's life, motivation and accomplishments as viewed by his son. Then a strange comment is recorded: "...when the opposition saw that they were not going to be able to defeat him at the polls, that caused many of them to feel that they should consider killing the man to have their way. Mr. President, I doubt that the man who appears to have assassinated my father would have wanted to make that move had he known or at least believed what Huey really had in mind." The word "appears" is a Freudian slip or catharsis, leading one to believe that Senator Russell Long indeed had misgivings about the veracity of the "people" who witnessed the happenings of September 10, 1935 in the State Capitol.

(Why didn't Senator Russell Long introduce a transcript of a coroner's inquest into the death of Huey Long? Was there an inquest or such a transcript? Would this not have shed light on the cause of death and the identity of the killer?)

And we can not forget that Russell Long's tender into the public record was made in *ex parte* defense of a man whose public service as Governor of Louisiana and U.S. Senator was tainted with accusations of corruption and dictatorial usurpation of power. In deference to the son, who injected his image of his father into the Congressional Record, nobody took "equal time" to dispute what was said by Senator Russell Long. And history, unaffected by filial bias and denial, will still be the final judge of Huey Long and his regime.

It follows that as the self-serving comments of Russell Long do not acquit or convict his father of the villainy of which he has been accused, neither does the transcript supply credible, irrefutable evidence that Carl Weiss caused the death

139

of Huey Long.

The preamble to the sworn testimony states that it is the "Transcript of Testimony taken before the Coroner's inquest held over the Body of Dr. Carl Austin Weiss, Jr., and conducted by Dr. Thomas B. Bird, Coroner of the Parish of East Baton Rouge, on September 9 and 16, 1935, in the City of Baton Rouge, LA."

Glenn S. Darsey, a Deputy Clerk of Court, certified the seventy two-page transcript before Lemuel C. Parker, a Notary Public, on May 5, 1949.

Unusual as it is that the transcript was not certified until almost fourteen years after the testimony that it recorded took place, this is no more odd than the fact that the transcript was withheld from general scrutiny until Russell Long chose to make it public fifty years after the event.

In his preliminary statement, Dr. Bird announced that the Coroner and the jury had examined the body of C.A. Weiss. They found thirty bullet openings were on the front, twenty-nine on the back, and two of the head, one penetrating the left eye and making its exit through the left ear and the other going through the tip of the nose and grazing the face. It is stated that it was impossible to tell which were wounds of entrance and which were wounds of exit.

Nothing is said about the make-up or identity of the jury nor of the place at which the inquest was taking place, but it has been reported that the inquest was conducted at the mortuary to which the Weiss body was taken. [1]

Two bullets were recovered just under the skin, one a .38 caliber and one a .45 caliber.

(If true, this proves that there were at least two guns of different caliber fired by bodyguards or police. It also establishes that if Huey Long was killed by a .38 somebody fired it other than Dr. Weiss. The gun which was in a sock in the glove compartment of his car, [and which is now on exhibit in the Old State Capitol as the alleged murder weapon] was a .32.)

A person reading the transcript for the first time would naturally assume that witnesses were routinely required by subpoena to appear and that nobody balked at the coroner's request for testimony. This could not be farther from the truth. When the 10:00 a.m. time arrived for the inquest to begin on September 9, 1935, no eyewitnesses to the shooting presented themselves. No explanation has been given for this, but it has been speculated that, since Huey Long was still alive at Our Lady of the Lake Hospital in Baton Rouge and would not expire until the following morning, Long's followers were heeding his command given the night before that nobody was to make any statements. [2]

The only witnesses who appeared on the first day of the inquest, the day after the shooting, were Charles Frampton (named in the Congressional Record as "E. Prampton"), a reporter for the New Orleans Item who was on the payroll of the attorney general and who was considered to be Long's unofficial press secretary; and John E. DeArmond, a supporter and bodyguard of Long—neither of whom claimed to have seen the shooting.

It is obvious from reading the transcript that the standard criminal practice of sequestering witnesses (keeping them out of the courtroom when other witnesses are testifying) was not followed at the inquest. Throughout the transcript questions were asked with the assumption by the questioner that the witness had heard previous questions and answers; and answers were sometimes given which referred to previous questions or answers. Failure to adopt a rule of sequestration in a legal proceeding allows for collusion and blurs the inevitable contradictions that allow the trier of fact to balance and compare, one with the other, the veracity and memory of those who testify. This results in unreliable consistency of witnesses, who assume the truth of facts recited by those who came before and, consciously or not, absorb these facts into their own memory banks and adopt them as their own.

The contribution of Mr. Frampton to the evidence is this:

He knows of only one shot before Roden started shooting. He says Weiss was not touched before the coroner arrived. That is doubtful. Even though the coroner, Dr. Bird, heard that declaration and later echoed it, there is no way that Dr. Bird can know that the body was not touched before he got there just because Weiss was face down when Bird arrived. Somebody had to remove his papers and keys for identification purposes and so that the Weiss automobile could be opened, ransacked, and moved as Tom Ed. Weiss said it was. In fact, the car keys of Dr. Weiss were never recovered.

Frampton talks about Weiss and Roden struggling for the gun, but does not say that he saw Weiss with a gun before the struggle began so, even if what Frampton says is true, it can not be assumed that it was Weiss' gun over which Dr. Weiss and Roden were grappling.

Frampton makes a definite statement that Weiss had a pistol in his hand when he went down. That, if true, is evidence that Weiss had a gun. But how could Roden have been wrestling him for a gun and backed away shooting if Weiss ended up with the gun? To accept this one would have to conclude that Roden lost the tussle, that Weiss could not fire the gun, and that Roden pulled out his own gun and fired as he backed away.

Supporting the idea that Long may have been shot by his own bodyguards is Frampton's statement that it is a miracle that Roden was not hit by the fusillade.

Casting doubt on Fournet's presence and his heroism is Frampton's statement that he did not see him at or in the vicinity of the shooting.

It is important to note at this time that there is no "chain of evidence," an important principle of preserving evidence, regarding possession of the pistol alleged to have been used in the shooting. Nobody knows why it did not appear in the photographs of Dr. Weiss' body. There is no evidence to establish who picked up the pistol, where it was taken, and where it was kept all these years. Also, there is no explanation as to why no effort was made to take ballistics tests on any bullets taken from Long's body in an effort to match them with other bullets fired from the Weiss pistol. With all of the bodyguards and representatives of the Louisiana Bureau of Identification and Investigation present at the shooting, it would seem that simple measures to preserve evidence and basic ballistics techniques would have been followed to establish that the assassin was Dr. Weiss, if in fact he was.

Many years later Dr. Weiss' gun showed up as an asset of the estate of General Guerre, the head of the state police in 1935. Nobody knows what happened to it after the shooting or, according to the Weiss family, after it was taken out of the glove compartment of his car. We do know that the only picture of the Weiss pistol in the police files was taken against a white backdrop and not at the site of the shooting or with the body of Dr. Weiss.

J. E. deArmond was questioned by Odom. He was in the office of the secretary to the governor when he heard a shot, followed by many shots about four or five seconds later.[3] Thus we have another witness who heard only one shot followed by a succession of shots

The most interesting thing about his testimony is the question asked by Odom.

"Q. Where the body lay, how far was that from the Governor's door?"

What is interesting is that this question is asked without any foundation or reference to the fact that there was a body, which is an indication that the witnesses are not sequestered. He was asked if he knew Dr. Weiss, even though the name had not previously been mentioned in his earlier testimony. He denied that he saw the shooting.

The inquest recessed at 4:00 P.M. on September 10 when there were no more witnesses to testify. Huey long had died in the early morning of that day.

143

The inquest was re-convened several times during the week to no avail, as nobody came forward to testify.

One can only imagine what was happening during this period. Did the Long forces gather the witnesses together to contrive consistent stories of the shooting that portrayed Dr. Weiss as an assassin wielding a pistol and the bodyguards as brave defenders of their leader? Certainly they took time enough for this to be done? Was the decision not to perform an autopsy on the body of Senator Long also made during this period? Without an autopsy the number of bullet holes in Long's body, the direction from which they came, the path the bullets took, the caliber of the bullets that killed him, the pistol from which they came and the exact cause of his death could not be determined. The effect of such a conspiracy would be to avoid inferences of culpability on the part of the bodyguards who fired their weapons and the doctors who treated and operated on the senator. The future of the Huey Long dynasty, the all-powerful, dominant political faction in Louisiana was at stake. The political and financial security of its followers would be in jeopardy. What greater motives are needed for obstruction of justice and perjury? Men have been killed, wars fought, and kingdoms toppled for less. The convenient victim of such a conspiracy would be a silent, defenseless corpse, convicted in absentia without a trial.

Finally, on September 16, 1935, eight days after the shooting, in the courtroom of the East Baton Rouge Parish Courthouse, the hearing resumed. The first witness offered was one of the important cogs of the Huey Long machine, John B. Fournet.

Anyone having illusions about the independence of the Louisiana judiciary may wonder what an Associate Justice of the Louisiana Supreme Court was doing consorting with Huey Long, a U.S. Senator exercising gubernatorial control over the State. Fournet testified that he wanted to talk to Long because "there was something I wanted to impart to him before he left Baton Rouge." He said he was following

Long when he left the House to get an opportunity to have a conversation with him about "two or three things."

Fournet was asked to relate in his own words what he saw and what he heard "immediately preceding the occurrence and what happened immediately afterwards."

Fournet says that as he walked down the corridor toward the Governor's office he met Joe Messina and they walked together down the corridor and saw the Senator leaving the House of Representatives and walking toward them.

Fournet then testifies that he saw this man in a white suit approach Senator Long and shoot him, after which Fournet put his hands on the man's arms and shoved him. At that time Murphy Roden began to grapple with the man in an effort to get his pistol. Fournet says he began to make an effort to grab the man when "they began to shoot pretty lively around there." The judge could not tell who, among the entourage, fired the first shot. He also gave confusing testimony about the number of shots fired before the barrage began and the time lapse between shots.

There is then a brief appearance by Gerald L.K. Smith who apparently insulted Odom because his statement appears to have been stricken.

Odom then begins his questioning of Dr. William H. Cook, a physician who participated in the surgery on Huey P. Long.

No questions were asked of Dr. Cook about the gunshot wounds to Huey Long or about the surgery, but the first question asked of him is if he noticed Long's mouth after the operation.

Dr. Cook answers "yes" to the question and states that Dr. Henry McKowen, who was giving the anesthetic, called the attention of all present to an abrasion or brushburn on the lower lip of the Senator and asked that someone put iodine on it. It was not bleeding until Dr. McKowen wiped it off with a moist sponge and then it did bleed just a little. In answer to a leading question, he said that it "oozed blood."

Gaston Porterie, the Attorney General, apparently unhappy with the direction the questioning was taking, interrupts and appears to be trying, by asking what could have caused the injury, to establish what did in fact cause the injury. The question:

"Q. Doctor, an injury of that kind could readily occur to any person after a person was shot who would have to take the steps from the first floor of the Capitol down a step of four flights of stairs to the basement and might strike any sharp angles or the marble in the Capitol after being wounded as he was."

Why did Porterie ask that question? Nobody had suggested how Long had injured his mouth or that he had injured himself while going down steps. Why would it be reasonable to assume that a person going down steps would injure his mouth? This illogical, leading question suggests that Porterie was trying to find an explanation for the injury to Long's mouth other than something which may have already been known, which is that Dr. Weiss struck Long with his fist. If this is not correct, then why would such a question have been asked in the first place, as it would not ordinarily be necessary to go to such trouble to establish that the injury to the mouth was caused in one specific way and, inferentially, not by another.

Would it not have been more logical for Porterie, if he was trying to be objective, to ask Dr. Cook if the injury could also have been caused by a blow to the mouth by a fist.

The answer, as expected, was that any contusion or trauma could cause that abrasion. And then the questioner says:

"Q. By trauma, you mean a lick against a hard surface?"

Of course the answer was "yes", but why specify a "hard surface"? Would somebody's knuckles be considered a "hard surface"?

Other witnesses then appeared but the testimony of all of them will not be extensively reviewed here. Among

146

them were:

Sidney Frederick the District Attorney of the St. Tammany-Washington Parish Judicial District states that there was a very short time, almost instantly, between the firing of the first and second shots. More time elapsed between the firing of the first two shots and the succession of shots that followed.

Cooper Jean says there was very little "space of time", if any, between the firing of the first two shots.

Ed Sharp heard the gunfire and estimates a very short period of time ("snap, snap") between the first and second shots.

Earl Straughan says he saw the body on the floor but is not even asked about a gun or whether or not there was a gun on the floor or in his hands.

C. A. Riddle, a member of the House of Representatives from Avoyelles Parish, claims he saw a pistol in Dr. Weiss' hands, with a "very bright barrel" three to six inches long pointed at Long. He says he was looking at Long and "loved him very much" and thought that this would be a good time to talk to him about speaking at a banquet in Marksville. He indicates that the gun was pointed right at Long "with both hands, if I remember correctly."

He did not see Judge Fournet there but says, "I heard him testify and he must have been there, but I didn't see him if he was there." This is further proof, if anything more is needed, that the witnesses were not sequestered.

He says that he thinks that Long and the gunman were about five or six feet away from each other.

In questioning a Mrs. O.P. Kennedy, Odom states that she was subpoenaed, which is an indication that certain witnesses were summoned by subpoena. I assume that this was done quickly if the hearing was to take place on September 9, 1935, as this is the date referred to at the beginning of the transcript. Except for Frampton and DeArmond, however, no witnesses responded until September 16, 1935.

The elder Dr. Carl A. Weiss stated that he was with his son and family much of the day, at the home of the elder Weiss and at their camp on the Amite River. They parted with the younger man and his wife at about 7:30 P.M. His wife phoned at about 10:00 and asked if he was at our house and he told her "no". She said that he had gone to make a call.

His son was very slight, weighed only about 132 pounds, and was 29 years of age.

He carried a pistol occasionally when he went out at night. He gives as a reason that they had been bothered by intruders in their garage.

Murphy Roden is the only witness to get a Fifth Amendment warning. (Was there some suggestion that he may have committed a crime, either in the killing of Dr. Weiss or the accidental shooting of Huey Long?)

He was an employee of the Bureau of Criminal Identification and Investigation. One of his duties was to stay with Senator Long and see that nobody harmed him. A State employee assigned to guard a U.S. Senator? Is that routine? Was this because Long was effectively performing as governor? Those questions were never asked of Roden.

Roden states that he witnessed the shooting but that he was not able to get the gun away from the man and he still had it in his hand. When Roden backed away he pulled out his gun and started firing. The man kept trying to shoot it and kept trying to work it around so that it would be pointed at Roden.

Roden was very close to the man and fired ten times. He shot the man to keep from being shot.

Roden is of the opinion that Dr. Weiss fired only one shot.

He saw Fournet. Confirming that he had heard Fournet's testimony, after being asked if he saw what Fournet did, Roden replies: "At the time he shoved us?"

There are a number of other witnesses who sing similar refrains. One, George McQuiston, refused to testify.

Another, Elliott D. Coleman, states that he struck at the man who "had the pistol but in the confusion my blow landed on some one else. I struck at him again and the blow carried him back because of the impact of the blow and the man who was grappling with him."

Paul Votier, appearing shortly thereafter, testified that Mr. Coleman "rushed in and punched at Weiss after Weiss fired the shot." Votier then says:

"Mr. Coleman walked in and punched at Weiss and, I think, struck Weiss and punched again and missed Weiss. I think he hit Senator Long in the mouth right where that bruise was."

Now isn't that tidy. Nice and neat. To explain the injury to Long's mouth, and thereby belie the fact that Dr. Weiss walked up to Senator Long and struck him and could not have shot him, Mr. Porterie gets Doctor Cook to state that the injury could have been caused as Huey Long was going down the stairs and struck any of the sharp angles in the marble walls.

Not satisfied with that, Coleman and Votier concoct a story that the injury could have been caused by a swing and a miss at Weiss by Coleman. The only flaw in the story is that Coleman says he missed Weiss the first time and when he did strike Weiss in the second swing the blow carried him back. Votier, obviously confused or forgetting the script, has Coleman punching Weiss first and then missing Weiss the second time and striking Long.

The problem with Votier's version is that if Coleman struck Weiss at all and the impact carried Weiss back, as Coleman says it did, then there would have been no need for Coleman to swing the second time. "Oh, what a tangled web we weave..."

Testimony on this second and last day of the inquest, in which 21 witnesses were questioned, lasted only two hours and thirty minutes. [4]

Is this long lost transcript the "official" finding of which Russell Long addresses the Congress of the United States? Can this evidentiary debacle, which includes no physical or scientific evidence other than the body of Dr. Weiss, be accepted as proof of anything? Can the coterie of Huey Long cronies, who poured out a litany of self-serving utterances in unsequestered unity over a period of no more than two and one half hours, unchallenged by cross-examination, be considered as reliable witnesses on whose testimony Dr. Weiss can be vilified as the assassin of Huey Long? If this is the case on which history has stigmatized Dr. Weiss and his family, then a whole new chapter must be written, exonerating the doctor and adding the question of the identity of Long's killer, intentional or accidental, to the unsolved mysteries of this century.

---

[1] *A Kingfish* by Ed Reed at p.27

[2] Ibid at p. 28

[3] Is this ubiquitous J.E. DeArmand the person bearing the same name who signed an affidavit as a room clerk at The DeSoto Hotel, attesting to the registration of certain named anti-Long occupants of the hotel when the alleged assassination conspiracy took place in July or 1935; and is this also the same person as Major J.E. DeArmond, referred to by Colonel Grevemberg, who "planted" a gun on the body of Dr. Weiss in an effort to show that Weiss had a weapon?

[4] Ibid at p. 31

Chapter XXV

Medical Appraisal

If Huey's diagnosis and treatment had been reported in detail, even reports of blood and urine tests, an autopsy performed, and a press release of details of his injury had been given at the time, little suspicion of deception would be aroused. No bullet was ever found, thus, for decades now, the questions of exactly what happened has intrigued many, including physicians.

Few knew Dr. Vidrine was a Rhodes Scholar. He did not act alone, but had Dr. Cook, who did most of the surgery, and several other physicians he no doubt consulted before surgery. All doctors were constrained from divulging details of the case by the doctor-patient privilege, legal obligations, political repercussions, and possibly, as with reporters, intimidation of a more serious nature.

There are no records of an x-ray, or an x-ray report on Senator Long. Could it be that no x-rays were taken? I am not sure. In 1935 x-rays were in routine use in hospitals in Louisiana. If I were to ask surgeons if they would operate on a case of a gunshot of the abdomen without an x-ray, the answer would be "no" in almost all cases. There is information that would be valuable if one bullet had entered and exited because it could be fragmented. The location of this fragment could be located by x-ray. It is often difficult to find a foreign body in flesh.

It is possible x-rays were taken and, "voila," one large caliber slug was found. If x-rays were taken and no bullet seen, then these x-rays may have been paraded before the press and photographs sent to newspapers and would appear in museums today! What is important in this particular political medical case is not what we are told, but the things we are not told until now.

Dr. Joseph Sabatier, who became a surgeon, was a

medical student at the time of Huey Long's surgery and was employed at The Lady of the Lake Hospital. His story is of interest and begins when he was walking with nurses near the Capitol after a movie. He heard a single shot, followed by many shots. In those days the windows and doors were open in the building and he first thought he was hearing a car backfiring. As they approached the hospital a single car drove rapidly by and was followed by more cars. When he and the nurses reached the hospital all exits were blocked by police who would allow them to enter only after being identified. He found a note in his room to report to surgery. Dr. Henry McKowen, the anesthesiologist, was very upset about the death of his friend, Dr. Weiss.

Sabatier agreed with there being two wounds in the colon. He did not know if the bladder was catheterized before surgery, but supposed it was done. As to x-rays, he again did not know, but guessed none were taken. As a medical student he was not privy to any medical consultation before or after surgery.

His opinion, then and now, is that surgery was appropriate since Huey was not in shock and significant internal bleeding was not diagnosable at the time of surgery. In those days most surgeons did not explore bleeding or a hematoma in the retroperitoneal space (area behind the abdomen and in front of the back). This could often cause more difficulty with bleeding. The bleeding was obviously known after surgery and was, according to Dr. Sabatier, the cause of death. Dr. Sabatier now feels that when more serious bleeding was expected or known the next day further surgery should have been attempted. The problem, however, was that no one physician was really in charge and doctors were a bit reluctant to step forward, make a decision, act on it, and receive the blame if Huey died. Could it have been known by the physician that Huey had a soiled bullet in him which would be a focus for further infection, making survival more unlikely? Dr. Vidrine, who had accepted the case from the beginning, was left holding the bag. He had issued the only bulletin.

As previously noted, mortician Merle Welsh described the details of the bullet holes. Ed Reed, in *Requiem For A Kingfish*, wrote an excellent account of this and also traced the bullet removed at the mortuary by Dr. Clarence Lorio. Welsh said Jack Unbehagen took the bullet. Ed Reed interviewed nephews of Jack, one a Mayor in Galveston, Texas. They recalled their uncle made the bullet into a jewelry piece and wore it on a chain, boasting it was the bullet from Sen. Huey Long. (The Starrs interview supports this.) Ed Reed's search for the bullet was unsuccessful.

Welsh noted the bullet hole in the back was small and "clean" which would indicate a wound entrance. Exiting bullets usually, but not always, cause more tearing of tissue and skin.

The widely accepted story in the beginning is that Huey Long died from a kidney wound, which was not recognized before or at the time of surgery. He subsequently bled to death. I know of three conflicting accounts of Dr. Jorda Kahle, the urologist in consultation. First, on September 9, Dr. Kahle was supposed to have catheterized the senator and found considerable blood in the bladder. The next account, which I previously heard in 1984, was by Dr. Hull who said Dr. Kahle aspirated around the kidney and found no bleeding. Dr. Tom Ed Weiss spoke to Dr. Kahle's son, also a physician. He claimed his father was minimally involved in the case, only peered in through the door at the patient and read his chart. Now, why all the confusion?

In the Louisiana Historical Quarterly in 1971, Dr. Frank Lorio noted in a bulletin at 5:15 a.m. that Dr. Vidrine stated there was considerable hemorrhage from the mesentery and omentum. This was the one and only communication to the public from doctors. Dr. Loria notes that there were two 'small' holes in the colon. The emphasis of 'small' would support a .32-caliber bullet wound rather than a .38 or .45. The fecal material the size of a bullet might suggest a larger colon wound or more soiling of the abdomen. Vidrine's one statement that there was considerable hemorrhage would lead one to believe there was more of a wound in the colon and abdomen. The famous surgeon, Dr. Maes, who reached Baton Rouge after the surgery (due to a mishap with his car), was approached by Dr. Tom Ed Weiss years later on several occasions. However, Dr. Maes always avoided speaking to Tom Ed. It was rumored in medical circles, in those days and for some time thereafter, that Maes did not have an accident, but delayed on purpose. One rumor was that the Baton Rouge physicians were told on the phone by Maes to operate in an hour. Maes, of course, knew it would take one and a half to two hours to get to Baton Rouge.

What is uncertain is how much the later consultants, such as Dr. Stone and Dr. Hull, knew of the entire facts. Nevertheless, they revealed little. Dr. Stone's critical attitude and his statement to the effect that Dr. Vidrine asked Dr. Stone not to mention the kidney are interesting. Dr. Vidrine would always be the medical "fall guy."

I am not sure which story to believe, but I'm inclined to respect Dr. Kahle's son's story. Further, if Dr. Hull did see a negative perinephric aspiration it helps to support the case against a kidney wound.

Dr. Hull was probably constrained his entire life and spoke little about the case of Senator Long. Dr. Harold Chastant, a relative of Dr. Hull's wife, who lived with Dr. Hull during his medical school days, told me that Dr. Hull was an exceedingly discreet man and Chastant thought Hull never had spoken to anyone about the case. My own guess is that Senator Long died primarily from moderate bleeding somewhere in his back, spine or retroperitoneal space, in spite of being given four blood transfusions. A septicemia from peritonitis developed which, without antibiotics, in 1935 sealed his fate. Also, if a soiled bullet was left in the body it would be a cause for additional infection.

Of note here is that a .32 caliber bullet, more penetrating, is likely to go completely through the trunk of a man.

This would indeed support a shot by Weiss if he used his .32-caliber to shoot Huey. A .38 caliber, especially in those days, sometimes did not exit the trunk of an adult. Further, it is extremely difficult to find a bullet in a body without the use of x-rays. Dr. Clarence Lorio certainly should have had the benefit of x-rays when he searched the corpse to find the bullet.

Several observed that Senator Long was quite unsteady on his feet which could mean a bullet may have hit his spine giving him not a paralysis but a "stinger" type of injury common to football players when forceful blocking or tackling stretches the nerves in the neck or spine. Jimmy O'Conner, nephew of the Jimmy O'Conner who met the Senator at the basement step, states that his uncle actually lifted Huey and carried him to a car. The driver of the car, incidentally, dropped them at the ER, drove off, and was never identified. Only three people were in the car. Many people claim to have been in that car.

Chapter XXVI

Guilty Until Proven Innocent
and the Victor Always Writes History

In preparing for writing this book I reviewed two history textbooks used in local schools. First is *Louisiana, A History* by Wall, Cummins, Taylor, Hair, Carleton and Kurtz, published by Forseman Press. In this book it is written "Shortly after 9:00 PM, Sept. 8, Huey stood near the governor's office in a corridor of the state house conversing with some of his followers, a slim man in a white suit worked his way through the crowd until he faced the senator. He then produced a pistol and fired one round, which struck Huey in the abdomen."

Another text, *Louisiana: A Study in Diversity* by Dethloff and Allen E. Begnaud, published by Steck-Vaughn, describes events this way; "Around 9:00 o'clock on the evening of Sept. 8, Long left the legislature and started to walk rapidly down the corridor of the new capitol building which he had built. His bodyguards scrambled to keep pace with him. Suddenly, a tall, thin man wearing a white suit and glasses, stepped out from behind a pillar. The man stuck a pistol in Long's ribs and fired one shot. Instantly Long's bodyguards fired over thirty rounds into the assassin."

So history is written. The problem is there was no trial, no confession. The District Attorney of East Baton Rouge Parish conducted a very inadequate and possibly a politically influenced inquiry. The pro-Long Attorney General, in spite of his considerable power, did not call for an inquiry and no indictment was made; nor was an autopsy done on Huey Long. Yet, Dr. Carl Austin Weiss stands in history as an assassin and murderer, indicted and convicted by history. No physical evidence was presented in 1935 or discussed at the inquiry.

There were two immediate beneficiaries of the assassination story. First, the bodyguards had drilled over thirty holes into a man who had no gun. They could have been charged with murder or manslaughter and would certainly have been ridiculed. Dr. Weiss was a small, thin man whom any one or two of the bodyguards and Bureau of Criminal Investigation officials could have easily subdued. The bodyguards also shot a prominent U.S. Senator in the melee. Equally important was the political asset of Huey being a martyr. The next election was four months away and the anti-Long opponents were widely and often referred to for some time as the "Assassination Ticket." Many voters could have turned against the Longs if a brutal shooting of an unarmed citizen had been known.

Dr. Carl Weiss's widow, of course, was seriously depressed and lived her life with the stigma of being the wife of an assassin. Years later she married a Canadian named Bourgeois. She was always devoted to the Weiss family and kept in touch or visited with them her entire life.

Dr. Tom Ed Weiss has spent most of his life trying to exonerate his brother. He related to me that one ranking official, who lived in those days, told him in strict confidence that his brother did not shoot Senator Long. When Dr. Tom Ed asked more about this he was told, " I know this to be a fact and leave it at that." The man was a patient and friend of Dr. Weiss. He was a confidant of Gov. Earl Long.

Also, Dr. Tom Ed was phoned the morning after the shooting. The call came from Brother Peter, who was the head of the Catholic High School in Baton Rouge which had been attended by Tom and Carl. Tom was told that his brother definitely did not shoot Senator Long, and that later the religious would explain to the Weiss family. He never did call again. Dr. Weiss saw him only once, briefly, years later and regrets he did not broach the subject.

It seems this religious figure had apparently negotiated directly with Huey for free books in Catholic schools in Louisiana. He had very close connections in the Long administration and was told this story. The Weiss family feels Brother Peter feared retribution against Catholic education

157

and had second thoughts about revealing this information.

When writing *Accident and Deception* I happened to see Morris Raphael, an author and columnist with a long career in engineering. He was working on a road construction project in the 1950's. He met a man who stated he was a Huey Long bodyguard and told the story that the bodyguards, not Dr. Weiss, shot Senator Long. Raphael said he thought this person worked for the state, but could not be certain of his name. There are probably many more stories like this.

I had an interesting discussion with former congressman Harold McSween, a participant in a seminar about Earl Long held at Louisiana College in Pineville in September, 1998. Earl Long developed dementia in his last term as governor. He then ran for U.S. Congress against incumbent McSween, who in his discussion was most considerate of his former opponent. At lunch that day, several of Long's close associates related to me how Earl took unrelenting cheap shots at McSween during the campaign.

McSween, a law school classmate of my brother Garland at LSU, was pleasant and informative in our discussions that day. McSween's father, John McSween, was the law partner of U.S. Senator John Overton (1933-48), who had been elected only through the support of Senator Long in 1932. Overton had expressed to John McSween doubt that Dr. Weiss was Huey's assassin, and supposed that shots fired by Huey's bodyguards might have hit Huey in the sudden confusion. For his <u>HUEY LONG</u> (1969), T. Harry Williams interviewed John McSween, who suggested others to interview. Harold McSeeen, who became acquainted with Williams while a student at LSU, drove Williams to interview several persons. Harold McSween recalls that Williams showed little interest in the shooting; and while on the State Board of Education with Merle Welsh (1957-58) heard Welsh relate the story of the bullet found in Huey's corpse.

Another interesting story is about New York Chief of Police Louis Valentine, who served under Mayor LaGuardia. Some time after the shooting, he happened to be in Baton

Rouge and met the senior Dr. Weiss, father of Carl and Tom Ed. Valentine and Dr. Weiss had only a brief conversation, but Valentine told the father that his son did not kill Senator Long. Valentine may have been involved in the Louisiana scandals in which 250 indictments were brought against Long associates. Few people today know that as a result a governor, an LSU president, and other officials were sent to the penitentiary.

I believe T. Harry Williams did a great disservice to history in the segment of his book dealing with the "assassination." He outright stated that the idea of Weiss not being the assassin was a "myth." Yet his coverage of the event in his book was very limited. All of the other aspects of Huey's life were researched and covered in tremendous detail by Williams. Williams also wrote a biography of Civil War General P.G.T. Beaureguard. His details, for example, of the Battle of Bull Run were remarkable. He had an amazing ability to research and write detail. Every order in the Bull Run battle was known and noted by Williams. Yet his treatment of the Huey Long shooting, the single most tantalizing event in twentieth century Louisiana history, does not rise to the professional level of this renowned historian. My findings show that there is no legal or logical basis to declare Weiss an assassin. Dr. Weiss was declared guilty without charges, but has been found innocent with an investigation into the facts. It is clear he did not have a gun on his person before he met his violent end!

Chapter XXVII

The One Bullet Scenario

When one considers evidence and statements in this case there arises the possibility that there was only one bullet. This is the one fired into Huey's back as reported by McGee and noted by mortician Welsh. There are other reasons to explore this scenario.

Both Melinda Delage and Dr. Sabatier stated no bullet was found during surgery. This casts doubts on the finding of Ed Reed that Dr. Vidrine's cousin, Coleman, had a bullet in safe keeping, supposedly removed by the physician during surgery.

I am quite impressed with nurse Utz's observation that she did not see any soiled clothes of any kind on the abdominal area when she was next to Huey's right abdomen in the elevator. Although she was nervous, it would seem she would have noted the clothing. A picture of the coat was found in the state police files found in the possession of General Guerre's daughter. This picture clearly shows the bullet hole and contrasting black powder burns on the light clothes. Had Huey worn dark clothes Utz may have more likely not seen this, but black contrasting on lighter material would have been easily evident.

The scrub nurse, Melinda Delage, did not actually see a wound of the abdomen, but admits she was busy with her tray and may have actually missed it. Usually, in surgery, the operative site is scrubbed and then drapes are placed around the area. There is considerable time when the site is exposed and it would seem that all those gathered around the table would have time to observe the site, even at a glance. Even such a glance would have left an indelible impression on Delage's mind, as did the lip wound.

Recall that mortician Welsh did not see a wound in the abdomen. He stated it could have been incorporated in "Dr. Cook's incision." Welsh here agreed with Delage and identified Cook and not Vidrine as the surgeon. Cook was the only surgeon called at the D.A. inquiry. Utz, Delage, and Welsh all thought Cook was an excellent surgeon, and in their opinion Huey might have survived had Cook managed the entire case. Welsh acknowledged that a bullet wound could have been incorporated in the incision which was in the right upper quadrant rather than at midline. He wished in retrospect he had more carefully inspected the incision. Dr. Sabatier stated to me that he did, indeed, see the gunshot wound in the right upper quadrant of the abdomen and it was incorporated in the surgical incision.

All of this raises the question: Could the "medical-political consulting team" have made a small incision in the abdomen to simulate a bullet wound before Huey was brought into the operating room and exposed to more non-political people? This would be very simple and could have been done within minutes. This is doubtful. A spent bullet may have been under the skin or recovered by Vidrine before or during surgery. Ed Reed claimed that Dr. Vidrine's cousin, Coleman Vidrine, possessed such a bullet.

Dr. Clarence Lorio, a State Senator, probably a strong voice, or even captain of the political-medical team, was not in the hospital before surgery. It is known that he was reached and awakened. He could likely have called the hospital and consulted with doctors and or politicians. Had Huey lived, would the name of Dr. Vidrine ever have been known? Would not Dr./Senator Clarence Lorio, a close political ally of Huey and ranking politician in East Baton Rouge Parish, have been a great medical hero?

According to Nurse Delage, Dr. Lorio took charge of the case during surgery. He told a doctor I have known for years that he (Lorio) pleaded with Vidrine to explore the kidney area. What spin control! Dr. Clarence Lorio held three part time medical positions with the state that paid him over $10,000 a year. He was a golfing friend of Huey Long and was accused of helping an electrical contractor pad bids submitted to LSU. He was convicted in federal court and fined $1,000. He was given a two year suspended sentence contingent on repaying the state $12,500. He had also been president of the Louisiana State Medical Society.

I have given much weight to Dr. Sabatier's observation of an abdominal bullet wound. The speculation of a fake wound became more alive to explain what Sabatier saw. If true, then the clothes with the bullet wound would also be faked. Let's think about this and question why, in the District attorney's inquiry, no one revealed these pictures or even discussed this evidence which was found years later. Also, if there were not two bullet wounds and two bullets in the body, or one bullet wound with one bullet in the body, and not a single bullet entering and exiting making two holes, why did the doctors in the operating room search for a bullet? Did they know a bullet was in Huey? Further, why did Dr. Lorio not search for a second bullet at the mortuary? Could there have been only one bullet?

Now what about ballistics in this case? I have consulted with coroners, a radiologist, and a forensic pathologist and studied forensic pathology and ballistic books. Their general opinion is that, not infrequently, bullets fired from handguns do not exit the body. There are many variables depending on the parts of the body such as hard tissue, organs, fat, and even skin. Often bullets are found under the skin of the opposite side of the body, having lost its momentum and being unable to penetrate skin which offers not insignificant resistance. Another factor is if the victim is relaxed or in a fight or flight mode. For example, a person passing by who is shot randomly is relaxed and muscles and tissues are not tensed. An individual in a confrontation has a body which theoretically offers more resistance to a bullet.

Of greatest importance is the caliber or size and speed of the bullet which determines the momentum. A rifle, of course, imparts much more speed and momentum than a handgun. Consider a .32 caliber. This was rarely, if ever, used as a military or police weapon. Any dedicated, intelligent, and thoughtful assassin would almost certainly use a more devastating weapon such as a .38 or .44. Weiss, it happens, usually kept a .32 in the glove compartment of his car.

Today a .38 or .44 would more likely exit. In 1935 the .38 and .44 caliber had much less velocity; however, the .32 had more penetration, but did less damage to tissue. I consulted Dr. Vincent DiMaio, a world-renowned expert in ballistics and wounds and medical examiner of Bexar County in San Antonio, Texas. He explains that a .32 does penetrate well but the .38 and .44 of 1935 were not nearly as fast or "hot" as the ones today. His letter is as follows:

June 29, 1998

Dr. Donald A. Pavy
P.O. Box 278
Lydia, LA 70569-0278

Dear Dr. Pavy:

This letter is in confirmation of our telephone conversation of the other day. In 1935, .32 automatic ammunition was loaded with full metal-jacketed bullets, usually weighing 71 grains. Muzzle velocity was 960 feet/second. If one was shot in the abdomen with such a bullet and it did not strike any significant bony structure, in all probability, the bullet would have exited. While this particular round is not a very high energy round, it is a good perforating cartridge. The .38 caliber ammunition in use at that time was loaded almost exclusively with an all lead 150-grain bullet. Muzzle velocity would be around 755 feet/second. If the bullet entered the back and traveled up-

163

ward striking the sternum, the probability is that it would have stayed in the body.

If one tried to put probabilities or percentage in regard to the actions of the bullets, I would say that for the .32 automatic with an abdominal shot the probability is greater than 50 percent that it would exit. In regard to the .38 caliber bullet, I would say that the probability with the previously noted trajectory is that it would stay in the body 75 percent of the time.

I really cannot comment on the .44 caliber weapons because I am not familiar with the type of ammunition that they used in those days. It was not the .44 magnum. It was probably the .44 Special. This was, again, an all lead bullet weighing 246 grains with a muzzle velocity allegedly of 755 feet/second. If there is any other way I can be of aide, please feel free to contact me.

Sincerely,
Vincent J.M. Di Maio, M.D.
Chief Medical Examiner

VDM:wb

If there was one bullet, such as a .38 or .44 (used by Huey's protectors), that entered the back, why did it not exit the abdominal area? Interestingly, here is the mortician's description of Lorio's probe into the corpse, It seems he reached up into the body "cavities" which would suggest the bullet was in sternal (breastbone) or mediastinum (area behind the breastbone). Bullets spiral like a football in the air but tumble more in the body tissues. They often take peculiar paths and angles in unpredictable directions. This bullet entered the

164

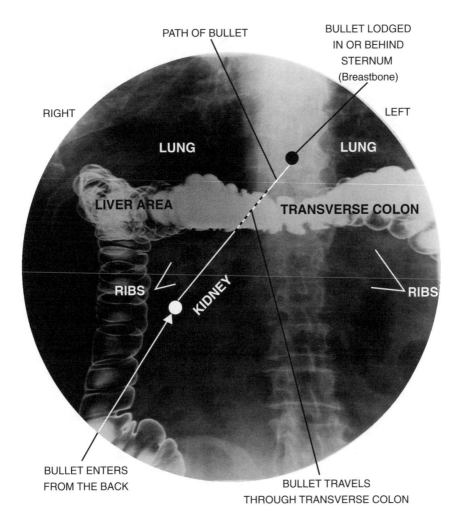

PATH OF BULLET

BULLET LODGED
IN OR BEHIND
STERNUM
(Breastbone)

RIGHT

LEFT

LUNG

LUNG

LIVER AREA

TRANSVERSE COLON

RIBS

KIDNEY

RIBS

BULLET ENTERS
FROM THE BACK

BULLET TRAVELS
THROUGH TRANSVERSE COLON

This x-ray demonstrates how the colon can be, and often is, high in the abdomen, sometimes under the diaphragm and near the lower sternum. The arrows demonstrate how a bullet entering the mid back just below the ribs, moving forward with a slight upward bias could travel through the colon and into the sternum. If the colon was higher than the entrance wound, an upward trajectory of the bullet would be logical. A trajectory to the patient's right would enter the liver and/or lung above it. A trajectory to the patient's left would enter the lung and/or, less likely, the spleen. A kidney injury would be likely.

165

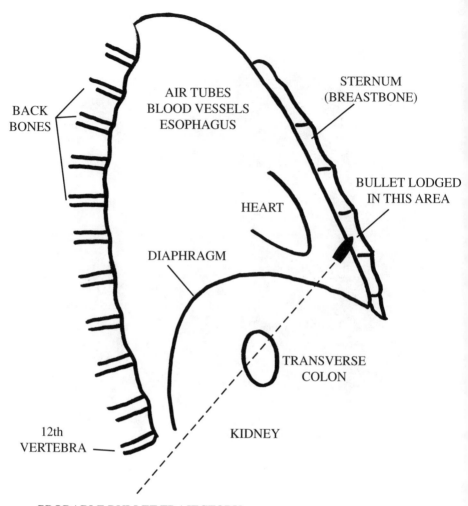

BACK
BONES

AIR TUBES
BLOOD VESSELS
ESOPHAGUS

STERNUM
(BREASTBONE)

BULLET LODGED
IN THIS AREA

HEART

DIAPHRAGM

TRANSVERSE
COLON

12th
VERTEBRA

KIDNEY

PROBABLE BULLET TRAJECTORY

This is a side view of the mediastinum or center of the chest cavity. It is the area between the lungs. The heart, air tubes, large vessels and esophagus are located in this cavity. The diaphragm separates the chest and abdominal cavities.

back, which has a very thick skin, heavy musculature and possibly a portion of bone (the transverse process of the vertebrae) the retropenitoneal space and/or kidney, abdomen perforating the transverse colon (upper part of the abdomen), the diaphragm and possibly the sternal bone or rib cage which it may have hit obliquely or tangentially which would offer considerable deceleration. What supports this is that the colon often is high in the abdomen. The liver often does not go beyond the midline of the abdomen. This would allow a bullet to slip into the mediastinum (area behind the breastbone) or sternum without injury to the liver. This location would have made it inaccessible from an abdominal incision. A chest incision (more risky in 1935) would have been necessary to get the bullet during surgery. A bullet which entered the anterior right upper abdomen, traversed the transverse colon, and entered the mesentery would probably not take an upward course. If so, it would damage the liver. Even in missing the liver, an upward course would bring it into the lungs. A liver or lung injury would not have been easily concealed. Also, there was evidence of only one bullet track. Another thought is that a ricocheted bullet would very likely not have adequate momentum to go completely through a trunk.

What about another scenario? Huey was shot in the back and then took a ricochet bullet as a result of the frantic wild firing at Weiss. This indeed would have explained the bullet wound of the abdomen. Ed Reed believes something like this scenario happened. Also, in the Grevemberg affidavit, bodyguard Joe Messina was distraught, thinking two of his rounds hit Huey. This is a remote possibility, but would indeed explain the anterior wound. The problem is, why was only Huey hit in such a wonderfully convenient location so as to align and match the wound in the back? Would fate be so friendly? Why did he not receive a bullet in the leg, arm, or hand? Also, why was Huey the only one hit by two wild rounds? One scenario could be that a bullet from the back could have gone all the way through the body, exiting in the right upper abdomen. If this were the case the statement made by the mortician, Welsh, who said there was a bullet in the upper cavity, and floor nurse, Utz, who said she did not see any evidence of a wound in the abdomen, would have to be completely discounted. Also, recall that Delage may not have seen an abdominal bullet wound.

This supports the belief that events were very rapid, and not everyone knew all the happenings; but one shot provoked all to fire at Weiss. Those protective of Long were not all well trained, if trained at all. Some had limited education and at least one was illiterate. These were not children playing with guns, but they were not anywhere near comparable to the secret service agents that protect the President now.

In conclusion, it would seem there is a good possibility that Huey was shot only once in the back. There may have been a wound in the anterior abdomen from whatever cause. This theory may well be questioned and I realize this position has limitations. It does, however, explain discrepancies. What raises the index of suspicion is that none of the doctors gave significant facts or details (were probably not allowed to) and refused interviews. Dr. Cook, a political neutral, refused to ever discuss the case. They could be hiding some things, otherwise, the Long family and politicians would have encouraged detailed medical discussions.

Chapter XXVIII

Summary and Conclusion

It is my contention that Dr. Carl Weiss had an inner seething to confront Senator Long and tell him personally how unfair he was to others, particularly his family. On the night of September 8, 1935, he passed in front of the capitol, saw an empty parking place and parked. He entered and went into the corridor where Huey was walking. Weiss asked to speak to the senator and was rebuffed by Huey who said, "Later." After the third very rough rebuff, Weiss, frustrated, lost his composure, screamed at Long and hit him on the lip. A scuffle occurred and Weiss was hit by bodyguard Elliot Coleman. One bodyguard, probably Messina (a nervous type), always close and often in the rear of Huey, pulled his gun, which hung up in the holster and misfired, striking Huey in the back. The firing at Weiss occurred from the bodyguards and some Criminal Investigation Bureau Agents, (the forerunners to the Louisiana State Police). Huey may have taken a second bullet from the dozens whizzing about in the small area. (This is highly unlikely.) Dr. Sabatier stated bullet fragments and powder burns were on Messina and Roden. He treated them in the emergency room the next day.

The bullet in Huey's back could have taken a tangential or divergent course or even been straight, doing damage to the back muscles and ligaments, and may have been near or hit the spinal bones. It could have lodged in the sternum or rib cage after perforating the colon. Huey was seen running from the scene by one witness, but others stated he was stumbling downstairs. His lip wound was noted by Jimmy O'Conner who met Huey downstairs and actually lifted him and carried him to a car. The driver, unknown to this day, drove them to Our Lady of The Lake Sanitarium near the capitol. Dr. Cook, a learned and experienced surgeon, and Dr. Vidrine examined Huey along with Dr. Cecil Lorio, a pediatrician.

No evidence exists that an x-ray was taken, but I believe most physicians would expect this as routine. The political associates of Huey dictated to some extent what the doctors would or would not do and say. The operating room contained more politicians and guards than physicians. Two nurses confirmed that Huey told doctors that Weiss hit him on the lip.

Dr. Vidrine may have found one bullet, but I doubt this. Dr. Clarence Lorio removed one in the corpse at the funeral home as the mortician related this to authors Zinman, Reed, Hair, and Professor Starrs.

Huey received four transfusions, which could have indicated shock from bleeding and/or sepsis from a fulminating peritonitis. Some people who are shot in an important artery do not live to get into the hospital. Others are given several bottles of blood to stabilize them for surgery. Long was given a total of four pints in about twenty four hours. He received, according to the nurses, a number of saline infusions. His corpse appeared quite bloated which could have been from excessive infusions given to maintain his blood pressure. In 1935 doctors did not have a good understanding of electrolyte solutions. Huey may have had a massive overload of fluids.

Dr. Hull refuted Dr. Frank Loria's claims and said Huey died of peritonitis. He was on the scene so I believe his opinion cannot be totally discounted. Peritonitis would usually take more than thirty hours to bring about death.

Meanwhile, back at the capitol, the bodyguards and their leaders were in a frenzy over the accidental shooting of a U.S. Senator and the brutal slaying of Dr. Carl Weiss. The doctor's name was obtained from his wallet, his automobile license was obtained, and a search was on for his car. Tom Ed's experience of finding the car with gun removed supports the Grevemberg claim. Within about one hour of the shooting, his car was found with a .32-caliber pistol in a sock in the glove compartment. This gun was placed on or near

170

him, but only after crime photos had been taken. Obviously the gun had not been recovered when these pictures were taken. Also, no crime photos were even taken of the gun alone at the time. What luck! The car keys were never returned, as were glasses, wallet, etc, to the family. In fact, the car keys were not listed in his personal effects by the coroner. How could Weiss have come to the scene in a car without keys?

Bodyguards had often abused reporters, so the threats of the bodyguards to the reporters were taken very seriously. Vernon McGee apparently was fearful for the rest of his life. The image of the riddled body of Weiss was no doubt constantly pictured in their minds.

A great disservice to history was done by T. Harry Williams when, in his book, he wrote that the idea of Long being shot by his bodyguards was a myth. Cecil Morgan's critique is thorough and challenges Williams' neutrality.

In summary it should be pointed out that the information that Weiss hit Huey in the mouth and did not have a gun is very strong. The scenario of the path of the bullet, at this time, may be less strong but good. A lip wound was conceded by all. Two nurses stated Huey told doctors he (Weiss) hit him on the lip. No gun was in crime scene photos made available to me. McGee did not see a gun. Brother Tom Ed's belief that the gun was removed from Weiss' car by someone else strongly supports the Grevemberg affidavit that there was a .32-caliber removed from the car by Huey Long's people.

In conclusion, I believe I have shown Dr. Weiss did not and could not have shot Senator Huey Long. His presence and actions did lead to the accidental shooting of Senator Long. Murder was never his intention. Being shot to pieces, of course, was also never his intention. He otherwise would not have driven into the empty parking spot in front of the capitol about 9:00 p.m. on September 8, 1935, to meet his unexpected, untimely, sudden, and brutal end.

I have done my very best to present the truth about the event based on discovered information and facts. I draw

171

obvious conclusions with no animosity and to the best of my ability. For decades the Pavy and Weiss families have lived in the shadow of claims that there was a plot to assassinate Huey Long. In particular, I wish the light of truth to shine on brother Dr. Tom Ed Weiss, now an old man, who has spent much of his life trying to exonerate his brother. He knew full well that someone other than his neat and meticulous brother had taken the .32-caliber gun from his car that fateful evening of Sept. 8, 1935.

Many persons could be inspired by the words of Msgr. Ronald Knox, a great scholar and writer, who wrote the Knox translation of the Bible. After his death the following was found among his papers: "What I have written does not belong to me. If I have written the truth, then it is 'God's truth.' It would be true if any human mind denied it, or if there were no human minds in existence to recognize its existence."

Epilogue

There is always hope that some day our government will officially proclaim Dr. Carl A. Weiss innocent of assassinating Senator Huey Pierce Long. Too late for Yvonne, now dead for over thirty years, to welcome such a happening. Hopefully, the Weiss family and their progeny, if God so deigns, will see this come to fruition.

The following are excerpts from letters sent from the widow, Yvonne Weiss in Paris to her sister in Opelousas.

Wednesday, July 19th, 1939

My very dear Marie,

Your letter of the 9th reached me only yesterday (Tuesday). Should have gotten here Saturday since it was sent by the 'Clipper', but the 'fete' of the 14th of July may have caused the delay. Anyhow, I was delighted to get it for I have had a horrible spell of the 'blues'. It has been raining continually, and now that Jeanne and Helen have both left Paris. I feel lost and utterly alone. I often think I must be crazy to separate myself from all of you whom I love so dearly, and install myself with almost a baby in a foreign country. I need courage for mine is failing. Maybe I am trying too hard, for yesterday coming home from the library at six, I felt so tired and lonely, I cried! Saturday, July 22nd, 1939
A very thoughtful young gentleman sent me two dozen roses last Thursday so that cheered me up a bit. I love the way Frenchmen sent flowers on the least provocation.

My blues have entirely passed. I try to

*console myself saying what a lucky girl I am
to have so many opportunities. When I finish
this thesis, I shall get a good position (so my
friends say), make a good salary, be indepen-
dent, and free to travel as much as I like. That
certainly should compensate for not having a
husband, home and children as I had dreamed
of having.*

Devotedly, Yvonne

Yvonne had difficulties in trying to leave France. Since
German submarines were sinking ships, the departure dates
and times were never revealed ahead of time. Daily she waited
at Le Havre to board. Suddenly, one day, the ship departed
for New York with her and Carl, Jr. aboard. On arrival she
called a Weiss relative who came to bring her to their home.
She had no money to stay in a hotel or even buy food.

Determined not to return to Louisiana to live, she lived
in New York where she raised her son, Carl. She returned to
Opelousas only when she became terminally ill. When she
died she was buried in Opelousas.

In Farmingdale, New York, where Yvonne worked as
a librarian, there is a library dedicated to her.

Passport picture of widow Yvonne and son Carl taken in the late 1930's. They were departing America to live in France to be separated from the stigma of her late husband being accused of being an assassin.
Courtesy of Dr. Tom Ed Weiss

To the reader:

An ongoing study of the Huey Long shooting continues and a second edition of this book is being planned. Any
story or information about the incident will be welcomed.
Please type and send to:

Cajun Publishing
2408 Darnall Road
New Iberia, LA 70560

References

Angers, Tom, (1993, Third Quarter) New evidence shows Huey Long killed by own men. Acadiana Profile,15, (6).

Associated Press. Bullet from bedside states Long's condition satisfactory. (1935, September 9). Morning Advocate.

Callender, George R., (1943, November 4). Wound Ballistics. American Medical Association: War Medicine, 3, 227-350.

Case # R1DO13191. (1992, June 5). Final investigative report: Senator Huey P. Long. Department of Public Safety and Corrections.

Cummins, L. T., Taylor, J. G., Hair, W. I., Carleton, M. T., and Kurtz, M. L., Louisiana, A History. IL: Forum Press, Inc.

The Death of Former Senator Huey Long. Congressional Record. Sept 10, 1985.

DeMuth, W.E., Jr., M.D. (1966). Bullet velocity and design as determinants of wounding capability: an experimental study. Journal of Trauma, 6, (2).

DeMuth, W.E., Jr., M.D. (1971). The mechanism of shotgun wounds. Journal of Trauma, 11, (3).

Dethloff and Begnaud, (1992). Louisiana: A Study in Diversity. LA: Steck-Vaughn Co.

Deutch, Herman, The Huey Long Murder Case. (1963). Garden City, NJ: Doubleday.

Graves, Daniel, (writer/director), Kingfish and Uncle Earl [video tape]. (This is a museum fundraiser production by Village Research). Winnfield, Louisiana: The Louisiana Political Museum & Hall of Fame.

Haaga John R., M.D., & Alfidi, Ralph J., M.D., (Eds.) (1983). Computed Tomography of the Whole Body. St. Louis: The C.V.Mosby Co.

Hebert, F. Edward. It was unbelievable; it was impossible; but Huey Long had been shot. (1975, September 7). The New Orleans Time Picayune.

Jeansonne, Glen, The Apotheosis of Huey Long. Biography. 12, (4), 283-301.

Jeansonne, Glen, (1993). Messiah of the Masses; Huey P. Long and the Great Depression. New York: Harper Collins.

Kane, Harnett, Louisiana Hayride. (1986). Gretna, LA: Pelican Publishing.

Long, Julius, (1933, September/October). What I Know About My Brother, Huey P. Long. Real America.

Long bodyguards and others tell of Weiss slaying in Capitol hall. (1935, September 17). Times Picayune.

Loria, Frank, M.D., (1948, December). Historical Aspects of Penetrating Wounds of the Abdomen. International Abstracts of Surgeons.

Loria, Frank, (1971). Senator Long's assassination. Louisiana Historical Quarterly. 113.

Marlin, George J., (Ed.). (1996). The Quotable Knox. San Francisco: Ignatius Press.

(1995, Fall). Kingfish in the Lake. Lake Echoes. Our Lady of the Lake Regional Medical Center.

(1993, August 22). The Baton Rouge Morning Advocate.

(1935, September 9). Times Picayune.

(1935, September 17). Morning Advocate.

Reed, Ed, (1986). A Requiem for a Kingfish. Baton Rouge, La: Awards Publications/Ed Reed Organization.

Roehl, Marjorie. Did the doctor do it? (1986, December 8). Times Picayune.

Stone, Duel, Conspiracy Unveiled. (1997). Monroe, LA: Lloyds of Louisiana.

Williams, T. Harry, Huey Long. (1969). New York: Alfred A Knopf.

Zinman, David, The Day Huey Long Was Shot. (1963). New York: Ivan Oblensky.